Unending Journeys
Works of Samuel Butnik

Published by ARTneo and the Artists Archives of the Western Reserve, 2015

Curated by Christopher L. Richards and Mindy Tousley

Introductions by Christopher L. Richards, Robert Thurmer, and Mindy Tousley
Essay by Elizabeth McClelland (reprinted from *Harmonic Forms on the Edge: Geometric Abstraction in Cleveland*, Cleveland Artists Foundation, Cleveland Ohio, 2001)

Design: Christopher L. Richards
Photography: Christopher L. Richards
　　　Page 9: Portrait of Sammuel Butnik by Herbert Ascherman Jr.
　　　Fig. 1, 2, & 4: Samuel Butnik
　　　Page 43 & 61: Mindy Tousley

Staff Support:
The Galleries at CSU
Robert Thurmer, Director and Chief Curator
Tim Knapp, Assistant Gallery Director

ARTneo
John Farina, Executive Director
Christopher L. Richards, Curator and Collections Management

Artists Archives of the Western Reserve
Mindy Tousley, Executive Director
Katelyn Gainer, Communications & Public Outreach Manager

Programming is made possible by memberships and support from:
The David Davis Foundation, Cleveland State University, Ohio Arts Council, Cuyahoga Arts and Culture, George E. Gund Foundation, Cleveland Foundation, The David & Inez Meyers Foundation and the Friends of the Art Gallery

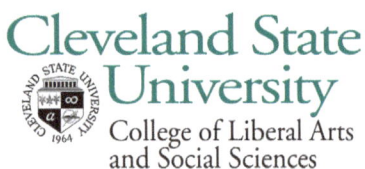
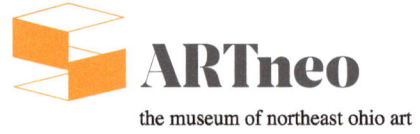
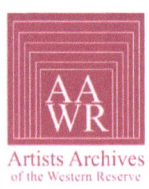

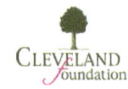
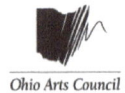

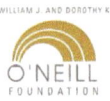

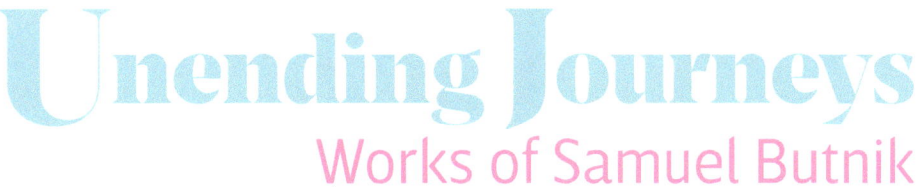

Unending Journeys
Works of Samuel Butnik

From the collections of ARTneo and Artists Archives of the Western Reserve

Samuel Butnik (1920–2004)

Presented by The Galleries at Cleveland State University
partnered with ARTneo and Artists Archives of the Western Reserve

1307 Euclid Ave, Cleveland, Ohio 44114

August 27 – October 3, 2015

Curated by Christopher L. Richards and Mindy Tousley
Essay by Elizabeth McClelland

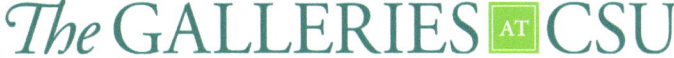

Introduction & Acknowledgements

It is with great pleasure and a sense of befitting gravitas that the Galleries at Cleveland State University present this exhibition of the works of Samuel Butnik selected from the collections of our partner institutions, ARTneo: the museum of Northeast Ohio art, and AAWR, the Artists Archives of the Western Reserve; two institutions with complementary missions, both holding extensive collections of works by Samuel Butnik, one of Cleveland's most interesting but least familiar great artists of the past Century.

This retrospective exhibition of paintings by the late Samuel Butnik traces the development of an artist with great gifts; a keen eye, cultivated intellectual curiosity, and an essential sense of wonder and adventure. Inspired by his extensive travels in the southwestern United States and Europe, Butnik used the genre of the landscape to explore both the inner and the outer worlds, which held such fascination for him. Using the landscape as a vehicle, Butnik was able to translate his experiences into insightful visual statements of great pictorial power.

A product of his time, Butnik came to similar conclusions as other artists of the period, who, striving to identify the essence of an image, began to abstract 'pictures' into 'visual ideas' in order to distill the character and meaning of the visual world. Over the course of his career, we see the inexorable movement from 'landscape painting' to painting the 'Landscape' – his methods extracting the most salient aspects of the picture – form is reduced and simplified, and color becomes complex, bearing the most critical ingredient of the visual experience.

Now is the time to reconsider the art of Samuel Butnik. This exhibition is long overdue. The Galleries at CSU are honored to present these paintings to celebrate the work of an artist who earns our attention, deserves the consideration of Art History, and merits the notice of the next generation of painters who will learn much by studying this exceptional Cleveland artist.

I want to thank our collaborating institutions, ARTneo and AAWR and their boards of directors for committing to this important project. I want to thank Christopher Richards for the perceptive and sensitive selection of works and for designing this handsome catalog. I want to thank Executive Directors Mindy Tously and John Farina for lending the objects. Special thanks to Gregory Sadlek, Dean of the College of Liberal Arts and Social Sciences for his continued support of the Gallery program. Thanks also to Marian Bleeke, Chair of the Art Department, The Galleries' exhibitions committee, and the Gallery staff, Assistant Director, Tim Knapp, Technicians Heather Moleke, Elizabeth Sisley, and others. Significantly, I want to thank the Ohio Arts Council and all of the funders for making this exhibition possible.

Robert Thurmer
Director and Chief Curator / Galleries at Cleveland State University

Unending Journeys emphasizes Samuel Butnik's ability to capture the feeling of the landscape throughout his career in a variety of styles. From his early landscapes painted during World War II, to his sketches from his European travels and his large abstract canvases, Butnik referenced both physical journeys as well as psychological and transcendental explorations. Samuel Butnik said of his works that they were an "unending journey of new images." The contemplative nature of the works allows viewers to become engulfed in their simplicity, wandering through the landscapes in their minds. This reflects his own penchant for exploration in both travel and new artistic ideas. Through the collections of ARTneo and AAWR, Butnik's fascination with color and form becomes apparent. Each development in Butnik's body of work builds on these interests. Unending Journeys succinctly illustrates Butnik's joy in those experiences and his desire to share them with viewers.

Through a generous gift in 2000, Samuel Butnik donated 175 works of art to ARTneo's permanent collection, consisting of early watercolor landscapes, ink drawings from his travels in Europe, and large-scale, soft abstractions of suns and moons. Donations such as this allow ARTneo to continue its mission of the preservation and celebration of the arts in Northeast Ohio.

I would like to thank Mindy Tousley, executive director of the Artists Archives of the Western Reserve, for her enthusiasm and collaboration on this exhibition. Combining works from both organizations' collections has allowed us to present a more complete picture of Butnik's artistic legacy and enhances the important efforts of both cultural organizations in establishing Cleveland's place in the history of art. I would also like to acknowledge John Farina, executive director of ARTneo and the ARTneo Board of Directors. Their continued support throughout the exhibition planning process has been invaluable. The support of Robert Thurmer, Director of the Galleries at Cleveland State, and the enthusiasm of the board of the Galleries at CSU has been vital in the planning and execution of this exhibition.

Christopher L. Richards
Curator and Collections Manager / ARTneo

The Artists Archives of the Western Reserve (AAWR) is very pleased to collaborate with ARTneo and Cleveland State University to reintroduce the works of Samuel Butnik into the public eye.

AAWR is a unique facility that preserves bodies of work created by Ohio visual artists. Its mission is to actively document, preserve, and promote the cultural heritage of the region through research, exhibition and education. The Archives owns over 200 paintings, prints and drawings by Samuel Butnik so when Christopher Richards and John Farina of ARTneo approached me about lending work to this exhibition I leapt at the opportunity.

In preparing for this exhibition I learned that Samuel Butnik was very reticent about describing his work in words and very little information has been recorded except that written by Elizabeth McClelland. What is known is that Butnik lived and traveled far and wide during his lifetime and each of these locations had an influence on the work he produced.

It is interesting to look at the very minimal *Phase* and *Circle Form* paintings done in the 60's, 70's and 80's and think about the influence of the New Mexican landscape he experienced while living in Taos from 1947 to 1950. The Sky Beyond paintings in particular remind one of slot canyons and the spare but dramatic desert landscape with its "big sky" effect. The sharp juxtaposition of color intensity Butnik was fond of in paintings like *The Sky Beyond #44* could well represent the contrast of a blue sky with the red rocks found in the desert. One can imagine the Circle Forms were the influence of the moon rising above a rock formation seen across a western landscape. Whether these speculations on inspiration are true or not, one thing that is obvious is that Butnik reduced his painting down to archetypal geometric shapes in order to play up his love of color. This masterful use of color is the thread that is found throughout the different distinct styles of abstraction that he worked in from the 1960's until his death in 2004.

Butnik was influenced by his contact with other Cleveland artists working in geometric abstraction, such as David Davis, who were known to each other and often exhibited together. Of these artists, Julian Stanczak, John Pearson and Ed Mieczkowski, have recently seen a national resurgence in their careers, making this exhibition of Butnik's work timely in reference to current art market trends.

I would very much like to thank the board of directors of the Artists Archives, as well as ARTneo, without whose volunteerism and support this show would not be possible. It has been a real pleasure working with Christopher Richards whose professionalism has been exemplary. Special thanks to Robert Thurmer and Cleveland State University for giving us the chance to showcase this work in a spacious new gallery and expose Butnik to a whole new generation of aspiring young artists.

Mindy Tousley
Executive Director / Artists Archives of the Western Reserve

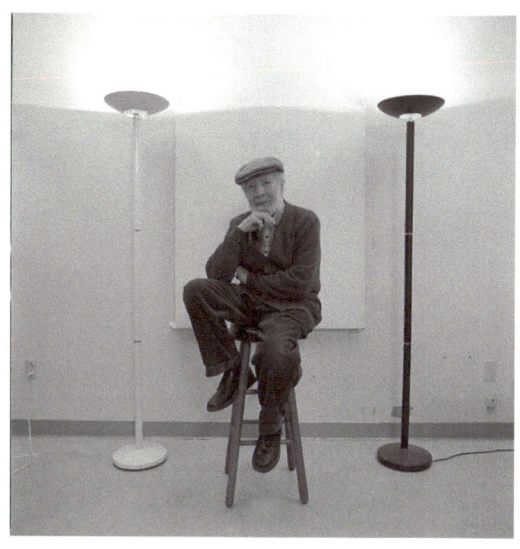

Herbert Ascherman Jr., *Samuel Butnik*, photograph, 2001

SAMUEL BUTNIK (1920–2004): DISSONANT TONES

By Elizabeth McClelland

Originally published in *Harmonic Forms on the Edge, Geometric Abstraction in Cleveland, 2001*

Samuel Butnik was born in 1920 in Cleveland, Ohio, and went to public schools there. He says there were no artists in the family and the only art that he remembers at home were reproductions of Maxfield Parrish paintings, which were very popular at that time. Still, art was the only subject that really held his interest during all of his school years. His parents recognized his ability to draw and sent him to Saturday art classes at the Cleveland Museum of Art. By the age of sixteen he was a competent draftsman. When he was a senior in high school he attended night classes at the Cleveland School of Art (now the Cleveland Institute of Art), studying figure drawing with Paul Travis. After graduating from high school he enrolled in 1939 at the Cleveland School of Art, but by 1941 with World War II on the horizon, he quit school and joined the Army Air Force. He was sent to the base in Santa Ana, California, where he hoped to become an aerial photographer. Instead, he painted numbers on airplanes, a job for which, he admits, he had no talent whatsoever. Despite his failure with numbers, it turned out to be a productive period and the Army, discovering his talent for drawing, used his gifts in a variety of other ways. He was assigned to drawing charts, and later to the Training Aids Department where he drew a number of instructional anatomical drawings. One was of two male profiles describing the spacing of the ears on heads of different contours. Another drawing with the slogan *"Less Talk...Less Dead"* (fig. 1) is of a living soldier standing near a body bag. In both instances his meticulous, realistic modeling delivers the required message. The artists in the Training Aids Department worked in a very large building, where personnel had access day or night, and Butnik used the space as a

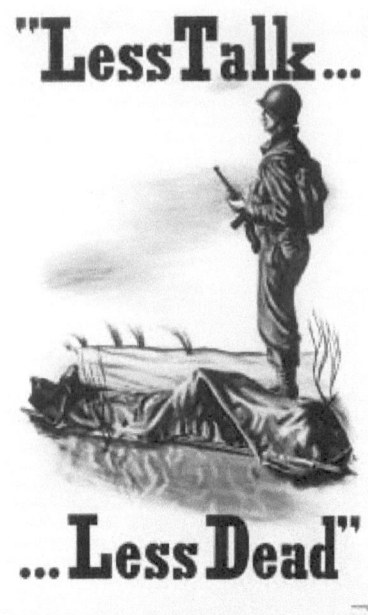

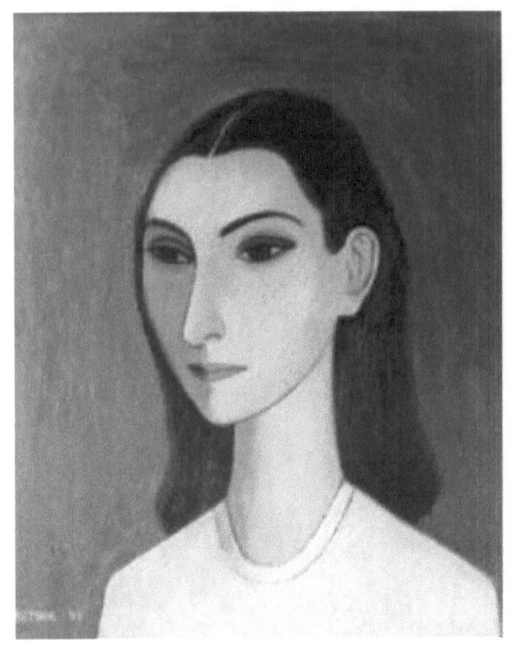

Fig 1. *"Less Talk...Less Dead"*, 1940s, ink, 5 x 3 in.

Fig. 2. *Lydia*, 1950, dimensions and location unknown.

studio in his off-duty hours. He painted a series of scenes depicting the vast canyons and open deserts that had so impressed him during his trip west.

Butnik, continuing the Cleveland tradition for fine transparent watercolors, was painting loosely rendered landscapes of the lush area around Laguna Beach. In 1944 the Ninth Service Command Showing of Army Art honored artists in the service with an exhibition in San Francisco. Butnik's realistic pen and ink drawing and his watercolor, both of soldiers, received a first prize and an honorable mention. After his discharge from the army, he returned to Cleveland and the Cleveland School of Art, studying with Carl Gaertner, Paul Travis and Frank Wilcox. He was seldom comfortable with formal instruction and pretty much went his own way, but nevertheless received his diploma in 1947. He then took off for Taos, New Mexico, where he studied art with the support of the G.I. Bill. He set up a studio and living quarters in an old adobe house and, as with all artists, past and present, he was impelled to capture the great beauty of that enchanted land. A realistic painting from 1947 is of a vast landscape with a wide sky and distant mountains. Two years later the conventional handling of receding space disappeared, and he interpreted the landscape by isolating its elements—a stand of trees, cattle grazing, horses in a field—within rough black borders. Even though the elements of the picture are not in perspective, their placement, their separation into bordered units, and their scale maintain the idea of open space. The rugged shape of the mountain reaching across a high horizon, and the colors, which are limited to warm brown, black and white, unify the composition. Although far from being representative, it is clearly about winter in Taos in a style reminiscent of Marsden Hartley's or John Marin's highly structured paintings of the twenties. (fig. 3) A portrait of Lydia was also completed in 1950 in Taos. (fig. 2) The stylized planes of the facial con-

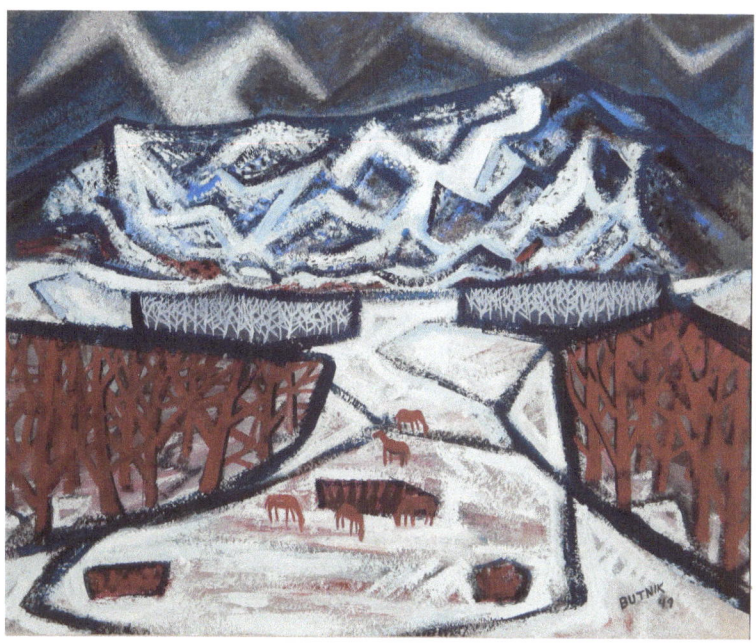

Fig 3. *Mid Winter Day, Taos, New Mexico*, 1947, casein on paper, 18 x 23 in,
ARTneo Collection, Gift of the artist

tours are a modification of Cubism and foreshadow the work he would do a little later in
New York.

In spite of New Mexico's enchantments, Butnik was drawn to the art mecca of New York
City and left Taos in 1950. His paintings reflect the geographical change; their content, which
is people, is tightly compressed and the idea of open space has been totally eliminated. He
painted from twenty-five to thirty portraits of people he saw in the subways and on the streets
of Manhattan. They all mirror the crowded places and the congestion of a big city. *Subway Stop*
(1953) could not have been inspired by any city other than New York. The heads of the subway
riders, one close behind another in airless space, are painted in still, warm colors suggestive of
artificial light. The man and the woman in the foreground are painted with a minimum of modeling;
areas of color and light and shadow define their faces in a mildly Cubist fashion, recalling the
earlier *Lydia*. The contrast between the paintings done on the East Coast and those done in the
West is as sharp as the wide vistas of New Mexico are from the structured canyons of New York.

In New York Butnik lived in a five-flight walkup on the Lower East Side near Delancy Street.
Two adjoining apartments provided living quarters on one side and a studio on the other where
he painted at night and on weekends. At first he thought about trying to earn a living with book
illustration, but publishers found his work too fine-arts oriented. Finally he took a job at a factory
which made shower curtains and where he "mixed hundreds of gallons of plastic paint for
the presses that printed colored patterns on shower curtains." This, he believes, sharpened
his natural gift for color and gave him insights into its vast potential. He found two galleries
interested in his work. Unfortunately, he decided on the dealer who was slow to introduce
his work to the public and shortly thereafter went out of business. The other gallery was

highly successful for many years.

In the meantime Butnik's enthusiasm for travel took precedence over making it in New York. By 1955 he had earned enough money mixing paint for shower curtains to fulfill his dream of going to Europe. He quit his "nine to five" and made it a point of honor never to work at a steady job again. *Samuel Butnik's Europe: Drawings & Recollections, 1955- 56*, is a book containing a collection of some of the drawings he made as he wandered through England, France, Holland, Sweden, and Denmark.[1] The drawings record the trip, avoiding the scenes on postcards and travel posters. He drew in simple lines with pen and ink, never working back into the original drawing. His eye and hand were so synchronized and the impressions set down with such fluency that they are alive with the immediate impact made on him by the particular place. Butnik returned to Cleveland in 1957 and concentrated on painting and selling his work. At this time he discovered acrylic pigments through the artist Anthony Vaiksnoras[2] who had brought the formula back to Cleveland from Mexico. Two works from 1958 and from 1959 show the influence of Paul Klee, whose work affected many of the Geo Abstractionists including Stanczak and Anuszkiewicz. One of Butnik's paintings with the strong flavor of Klee, *Sounds of Night*, done in acrylic, received first prize in painting in the forty-first Cleveland Museum of Art *May Show*. The other, *Composition #10*, a mixed-media drawing, was purchased for the museum by the Institute of Decorators from the 1958 May Show. In the early 1960s Butnik's paintings were leaning more and more toward what he calls "soft abstraction." Working in acrylic as well as oil in modulated colors, his forms were often amorphous but never expressionistic. *Image #4* and *Juxtaposition Red*, both from the later 1950s, were tightly composed of large, roughly rectangular, often overlapping shapes. When they were shown in the big national exhibition in New York City called *Art USA '58*, Emily Genauer, the art critic for the New York *Herald Tribune* bought *Juxtaposition Red* from the show. At this period of his career, distinguished collectors, private and corporate, were becoming interested in Butnik's strong and colorful abstractions. In 1964 Butnik received a letter from Sherman E. Lee, then the director of the Cleveland Museum of Art, requesting his permission to circulate his painting *Distant Storm* in an exhibition traveling throughout the United States.[3] The jury had rejected this painting for inclusion in the *May Show*. Dr. Lee said in his letter, "In reviewing the entries submitted to this year's *May Show*, many of us liked your work very much and felt it was of more than local interest," thereby refuting the ironclad expertise of jurors for competitive exhibitions. The painting is of rough water and a surly red sky with streaks of dark clouds announcing a coming storm. It was one of a series motivated by viewing Lake Erie in its different moods while driving on the shoreway. In the flourishes of the brushwork, it comes close to Abstract Expressionism, but circumvents it because of its simplicity and semblance of realism.

Butnik says that the change that occurred in his work a few years later was triggered by a documentary film on Stonehenge in 1966. Inspired by the huge stone shapes with the light

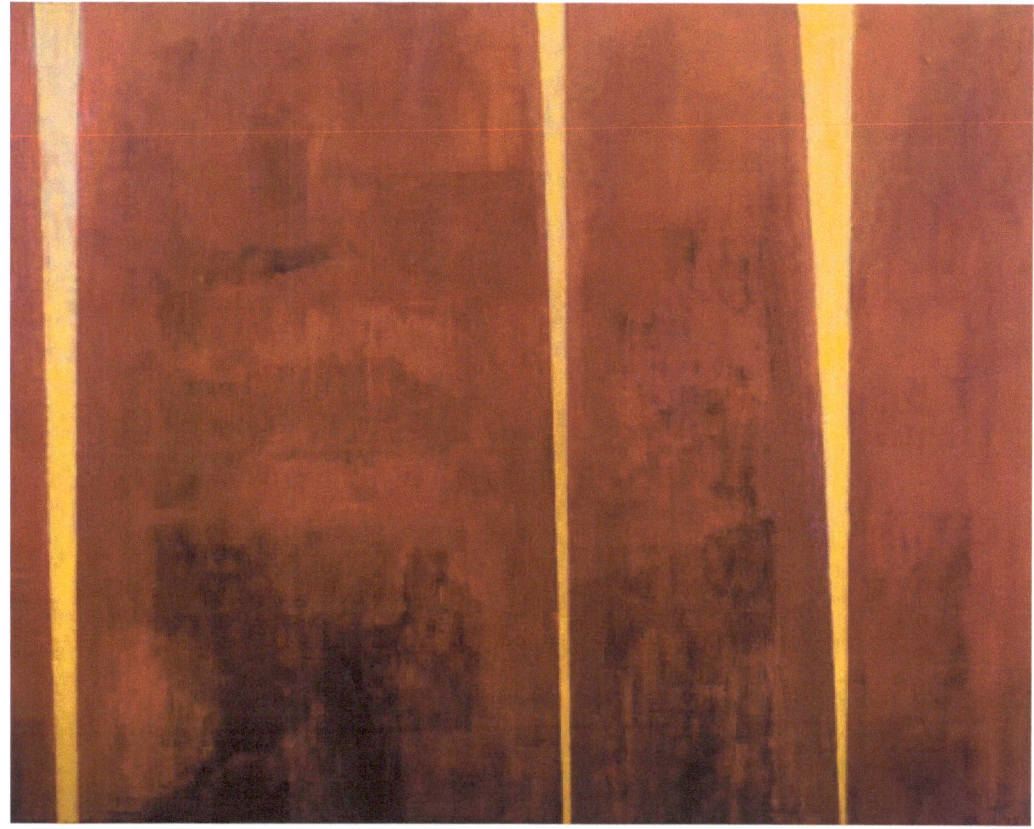

Fig 4. *Stonehenge I*, 1966, acrylic on canvas, 37 x 47 in, location unknown.

behind them outlining their rugged contours, he went to the studio the next day and began creating the large, clearly-defined forms of his *Stonehenge Series*. In *Stonehenge I*, (fig. 4) the thick vertical shapes, imprecise in configuration and unevenly spaced, resemble the source of their inspiration. As the series progressed, he refined the forms and evened the edges. They laid the foundation for his hard-edged paintings of the late 1960s and 1970s when their tonalities would become vibrant. With the use of acrylic paint and tape to achieve the desired precision, he exploited abstract shapes—ovals, spheres, Xs, Vs, rectangles, and ellipses—large enough to carry offbeat and pure colors effectively.

Except for his early paintings done in Taos, New Mexico, color has always been the most important element in Butnik's work. Ad Reinhardt, famous for his black on black paintings, said, "There is something wrong, irresponsible and mindless about color, something impossible to control."[4] Certainly, color has a life of its own and one color interacting with others simply increases that irresponsibility. Controlling its behavior, making it do their bidding has obsessed artists throughout the centuries. While Reinhardt in the 1960s was taking painting to the ultimate end with his black on black compositions, many artists were reducing their work to nonobjectivity featuring color. As Reinhardt eliminated the color/non-color problem, anticipating the utmost extreme of Minimalism, art publications were filled with essays dealing with color on stained canvases, shaped paintings, saturated fields and Op Art. Op, concerned with color theory, was at its peak with

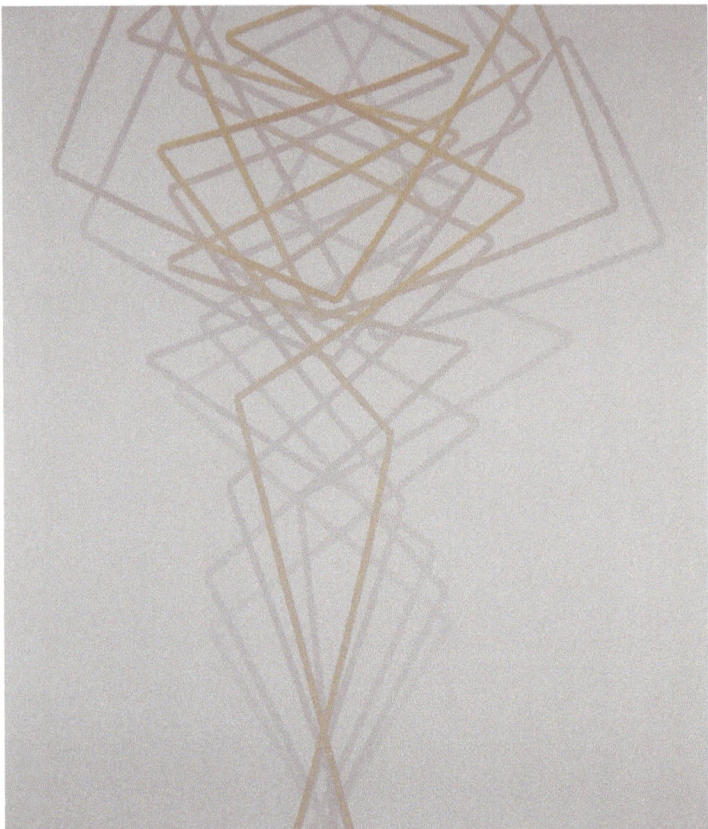

Fig 4. *Configuration Series III, Grey 5*, 1975, acrylic on canvas, 60 x 48 in., Artists Archives of the Western Reserve

dizzying and dazzling creations. No matter how much they varied stylistically, the artists' common goal was painting itself.

Butnik's preoccupation was with large forms saturated with colors that sometimes lost their identity in their complex mix. The consistency of acrylic paint permitted various ways of applying it with brush, roller or sponge. And with its fast drying time it could be readily layered so that underlying colors would effect the subtlety of the final color. Enthralled with these possibilities he painted large and small circles that look as though they might roll up or down a curve of color and out into space. A slice of color on one form is continued on another. A big circle is interrupted by the intrusion of an inverted sphere. Shapes touch and glance off one another. There is often the implication that the painting is completed somewhere off the canvas. Colors are played against one another: a sullen ochre pushes against reddish purple. Rusty reds, bright magentas, vibrant blues, sweet and sour, lively and quiet, coexist in a state of splendid dissonance. Forms of subtle and unusual color combinations are arranged in positions of precarious balance.

For these paintings Butnik made small rough sketches on graph paper and transferred them enlarged to the scale of the size of the canvas. He used color pure and mixed but never a conjunction of primary colors, so instead of the vibration that occurs when primary colors meet, there is a slight frisson where the edge of one hue abuts another. Mixing two or three or more colors, he would test them over and over until he found just the shade he wanted. He then prepared enough paint and stored it in large and small jars so that he wouldn't be in danger of running out until the painting was finished. At times he mixed aluminum pigment in the paint and applied it with a textured roller so the painting's surface glistened slightly as though a light frost had settled on it.

Often one shape nearly fills the canvas, and its color derives its effulgence from the small visible field or background; without framing of any sort the painting appears to be completed somewhere "out there." The forms are positioned precariously. A circle appears to be rolling off canvas. Or a white X is so shaped as to be heavier at the top than at the bottom and thus causes tension. With forms that are off balance or moving beyond the canvas, plus colors that cannot be positively identified, Butnik's concept might be ambiguity. In 1966 Nicholas Livaich, who was the director of the now defunct Cooper School of Art, said in a statement announcing an exhibition of Butnik's paintings that they were a "feast of opulent color" and of a "subtle contemplative nature." Butnik, sounding a little like Frank Stella, said there was no point in moving close to look at his paintings because, "There's nothing to see up close."[5] That is true. The enigmatic presence of the paintings is best experienced by lingering at a short distance from them. During this period Butnik was active in Ohio's art scene, as an exhibiting artist and as a member of the Ohio Arts Council Visual Arts Advisory Panel. His work was receiving favorable attention from jurors of competitive exhibitions and from collectors. He was also teaching private classes in his studio on Coventry Road in Cleveland Heights. Butnik and other artists in Cleveland were enjoying a renaissance of sorts in the visual arts during the 1970s and early 1980s. Despite this relatively congenial atmosphere, Butnik left Cleveland in 1971 for Providence, Rhode Island. For the next five years he painted and exhibited on the East Coast, but he was out of touch with the art world of Northeast Ohio. When he returned to Ohio, his paintings were undergoing a change. The component shapes were smaller and sharper and the rhythm was faster. In the *Configuration Series* (1974–1978) (fig. 5) the movement that was impending before in the large forms is now animated. The earliest works of this series are composed of short bands of color, streaking across the canvas like tossed jackstraws, forming triangles and rhomboids where they meet. Each band is painted a solid color; when rosy red bands are placed on hot purple fields, the radiance presses forward heating up the painting's total surface and the space beyond it. As the series progressed Butnik tested his ability to make imperceptible tonal changes in the lines. The later paintings show one continuous line; starting at the top of the canvas, he pulls the line out at sharp angles to the right and crosses it sharply to the left, tapering it towards the bottom. The configuration, narrow at the top and at the bottom, is widest near the middle of the canvas. Its colors change subtly as the crisscrossing bands zigzag downward forming triangular negative shapes. By 1976 the cool tones are dominant (and all but impossible to reproduce): in one such painting silver grays, creamy tans, beiges and steely greens are carefully modulated, graded imperceptibly from one color and tone into another. The cool and warm tones move back and forth like a dancer on a pale, bare stage. At its widest point the configuration resembles the sharp edges of a dancer's tutu; the form, which was also compared to a whirling dervish, finally ends on point. With the reduction of color, there remains just enough tonal change within the lines to engage the eye in the complexity of the lines' rhythm. Now, unlike the big solid shapes, there are subtleties to see by moving closer. Because of the narrowness of the bands and the blending of colors these paintings are perhaps the most technically demanding of all his work, and required a painstaking method. First he applied the ground (flat white) and when that dried he "drew" his composition with narrow tape applied to the canvas; he then painted the whole surface a solid background color. After a drying period, he would pull off the tape and follow the lines, carefully grading one tone into another as he painted. From 1980-81 he also produced some of his most exciting hard-edge paintings. The forms were larger and bolder and the colors were stronger and even more subtle than those from the earlier period. However, failing eyesight was making meticulous edges and finely blended colors exceedingly difficult to achieve. Seeking another way of working, he explored the possibilities of minimal landscapes and developed a truly original way of producing monotypes. By the 1990s, he returned to oil paint and lyrical interacting spheres. The first of these paintings from 1989-91 are smaller and gentler in color than anything he had done before. When he began this group, Butnik said, "Paintings for the twenty-first century." Thinking in terms of the exploding population and the analogous decrease in private space, the paintings were smaller to fit what he thought was the situation. Although the construction of outsized houses continues unabated, Butnik's logical but faulty reasoning produced some beautiful oil paintings. They have since grown in size and intensity of color. Looking at them, one cannot help but think of Delaunay's *Disques and Formes Circulaires Cosmiques* of 1912 and of *Orphism*.[6] They are the embodiment of light and color and motion. The spherical shapes in clear, ingratiating colors interlock as they float on the surface of the canvas. Butnik has combined features of previous work: circles, traversing bands of color. But where the static forms appear to anticipate movement (the circle might roll away or two shapes might squeeze the middle one) in his hard-edged canvases, here the merging colors float gracefully in their own cosmos. In 1997, Butnik returned to the "jackstraws" with colored inks on paper. The "straws" were not pre-planned and their development was similar to Pollock's drip paintings. The artist putting down the colors/lines in reciprocal arrangements relying on intuition, guided, of course, by experience. By controlling the color, length, direction, and number of lines, Butnik arrived at exuberant compositions filled with lively movement. And, although Butnik's "jackstraws" are conceived on a much smaller scale than Pollock's drip paintings or John Pearson's *Mondrian Series*, the viewer is still drawn into the painting's fictitious depth. The lines streak over the surface, causing positive and negative configurations that are fun to follow.

Except for conversations with interviewers, Sam Butnik has said very little about his work, and he has written even less. His theories and concepts are worked out on canvas or paper; he believes that you either understand what he has done or you don't. In a statement for the exhibition *Midwest Painters Invitational* he pointed out that his painting, in rejecting nostalgia, sentiment, and myth, was an effort toward the "realization of new experiences." It is obvious from some of the early work that he looked as hard at Paul Klee as he did at the Stonehenge documentary. He has always been an acute observer of things, especially paintings, and was aware of the myriad styles that followed the Abstract Expressionists. Out of the heady mix, he developed his way of expressing what interested him most—forms to convey the excitement of color for its own sake without adhering to any theory. Looking at any of Butnik's solo exhibitions there is no question of color's imperative. An exceptionally fine installation at Ashland University's Coburn Gallery in 1992 was a retrospective of two decades of Butnik's work from the carefully plotted big forms to the random, intuitive compositions. Forms in opulent colors, pure and mixed, held in perilous equilibrium made the gallery positively glow.

NOTES
1. Samuel Butnik. *Samuel Butnik's Europe: Drawings & Recollections - 1955-56.* Introduction, Elizabeth McClelland. OHIO ARTISTS NOW, Cleveland, OH. 1994
2. Anthony Vaiksnoras was a well-known painter of the Cleveland School. He traveled and painted in Mexico and on one occasion returned to Ohio with the then new formula for acrylic paint.
3. The Cleveland Museum of Art organized a yearly traveling show consisting of works by *May Show* exhibitors. The exhibit traveled to small museums and universities throughout the United States. In 1964 they made a wise exception (based on the museum's demands of quality instead of the jury's) and included Butnik's painting.
4. Ad Reinhardt was called the "black monk" partly because of his black on black paintings, and also because of his unswerving faith in his own aesthetic and his acerbic and often witty writings on his personal "theology."
5. Samuel Butnik in "The Minimal Artists," by Owen Findsen in the Cincinnati Enquirer, July 7, 1968. In 1964, Frank Stella being interviewed by Bruce Glaser on radio WBAI-FM, NY, said "What you see is what you see."
6. Robert Delaunay believed that light and color were identical and that colors create movement. His pure painting was without reference to anything except color and its rhythmical effects. Delaunay's friend, the poet Apollinaire, named the painting style Orphic Cubism.
7. *Midwest Painters Invitational*, Grand Rapids Art Gallery, Grand Rapids, Michigan, 1960. Julian Stanczak was also an exhibitor in this show.

Plates

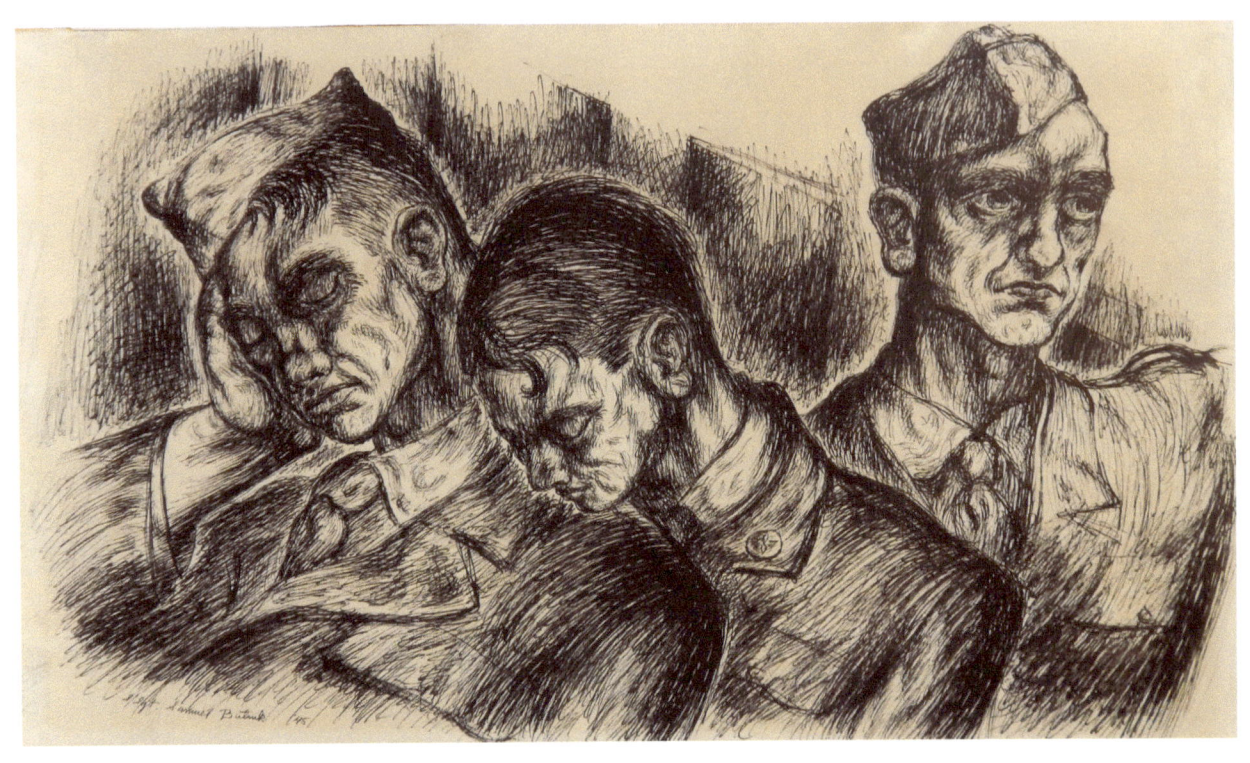

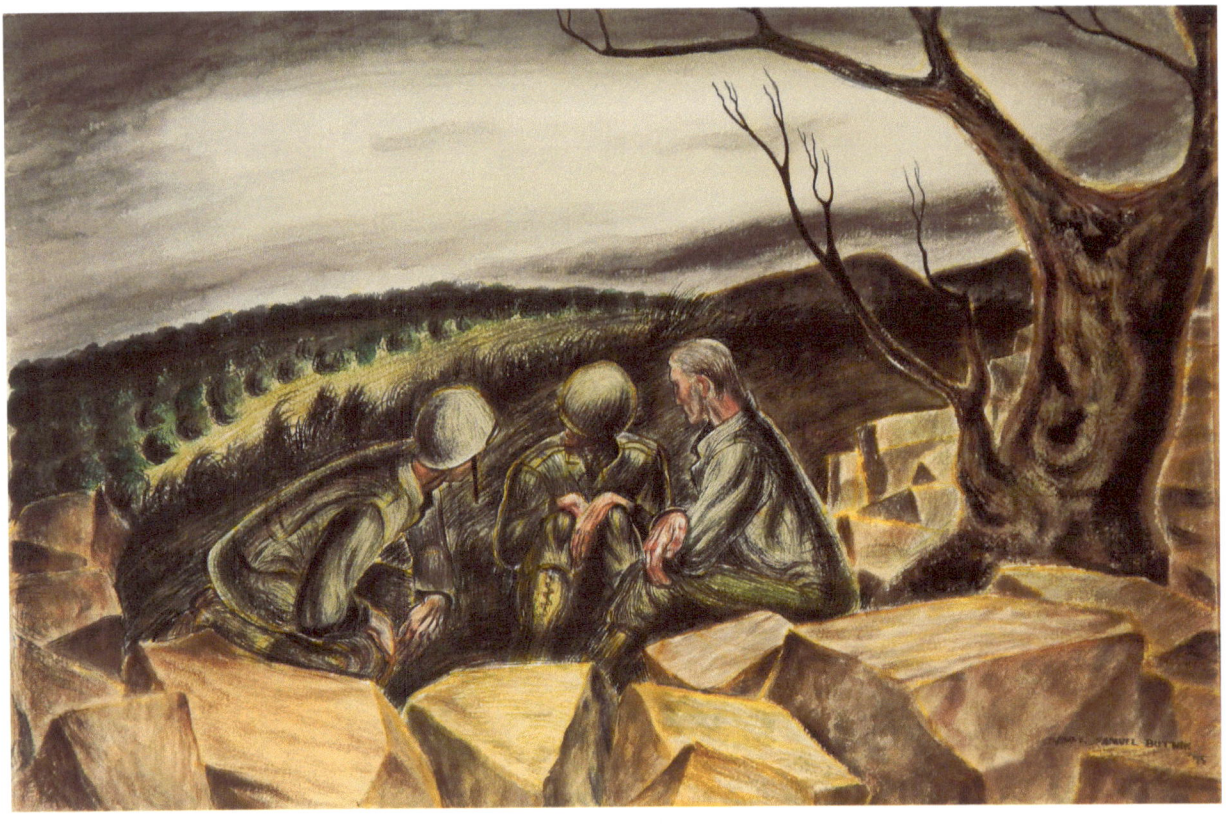

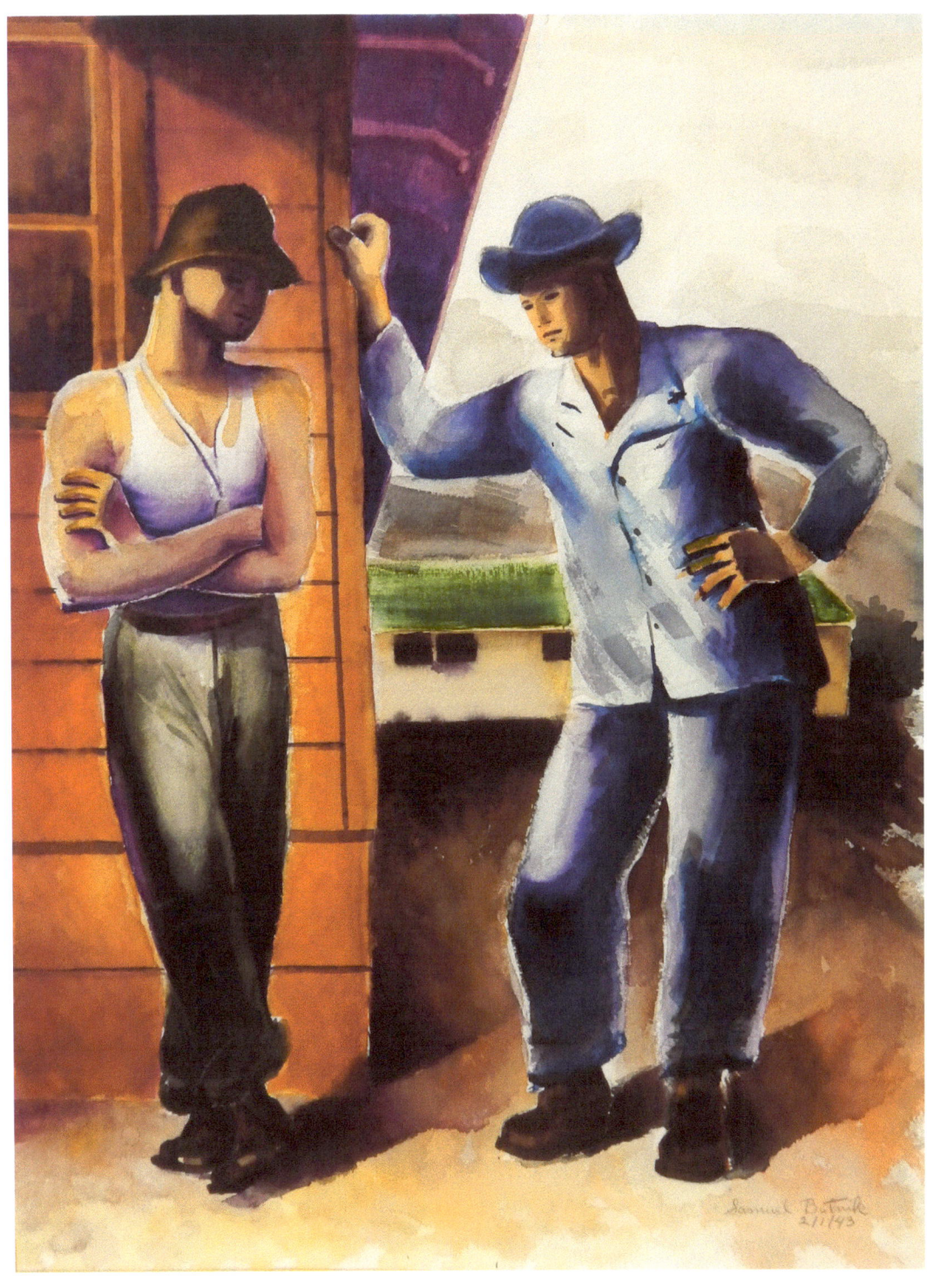

Opposite:
Streetcar to Santa Ana, 1945
Ink on board, 11 x 19 in.
ARTneo Collection, Gift of the artist

Army 1945, 1945
Ink, watercolor on paper, 15 x 23 in.
ARTneo Collection, Gift of the artist

At Ease, 1943
Watercolor on paper, 18 x 13.75 in.
ARTneo Collection, Gift of the artist

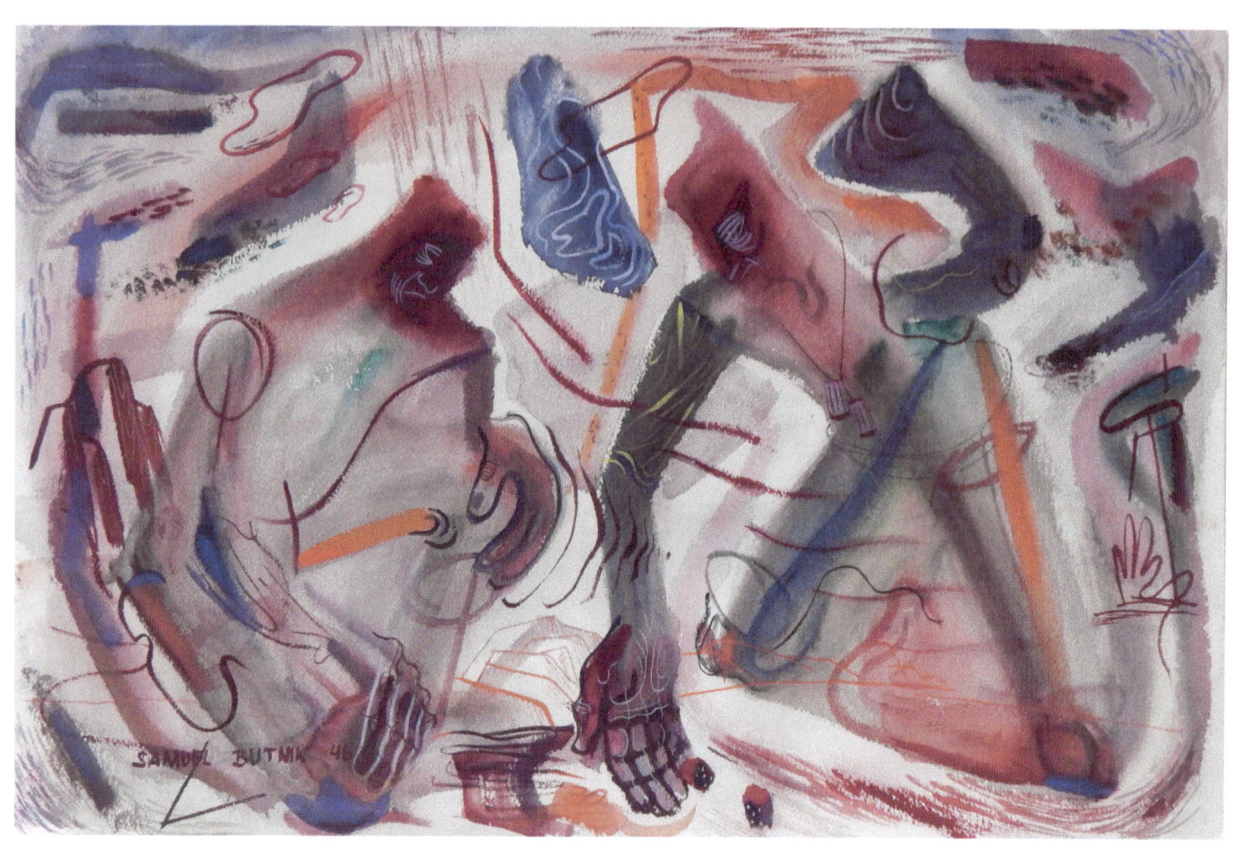

Chance, 1946
Watercolor on paper, 15 x 23 in.
ARTneo Collection, Gift of the artist

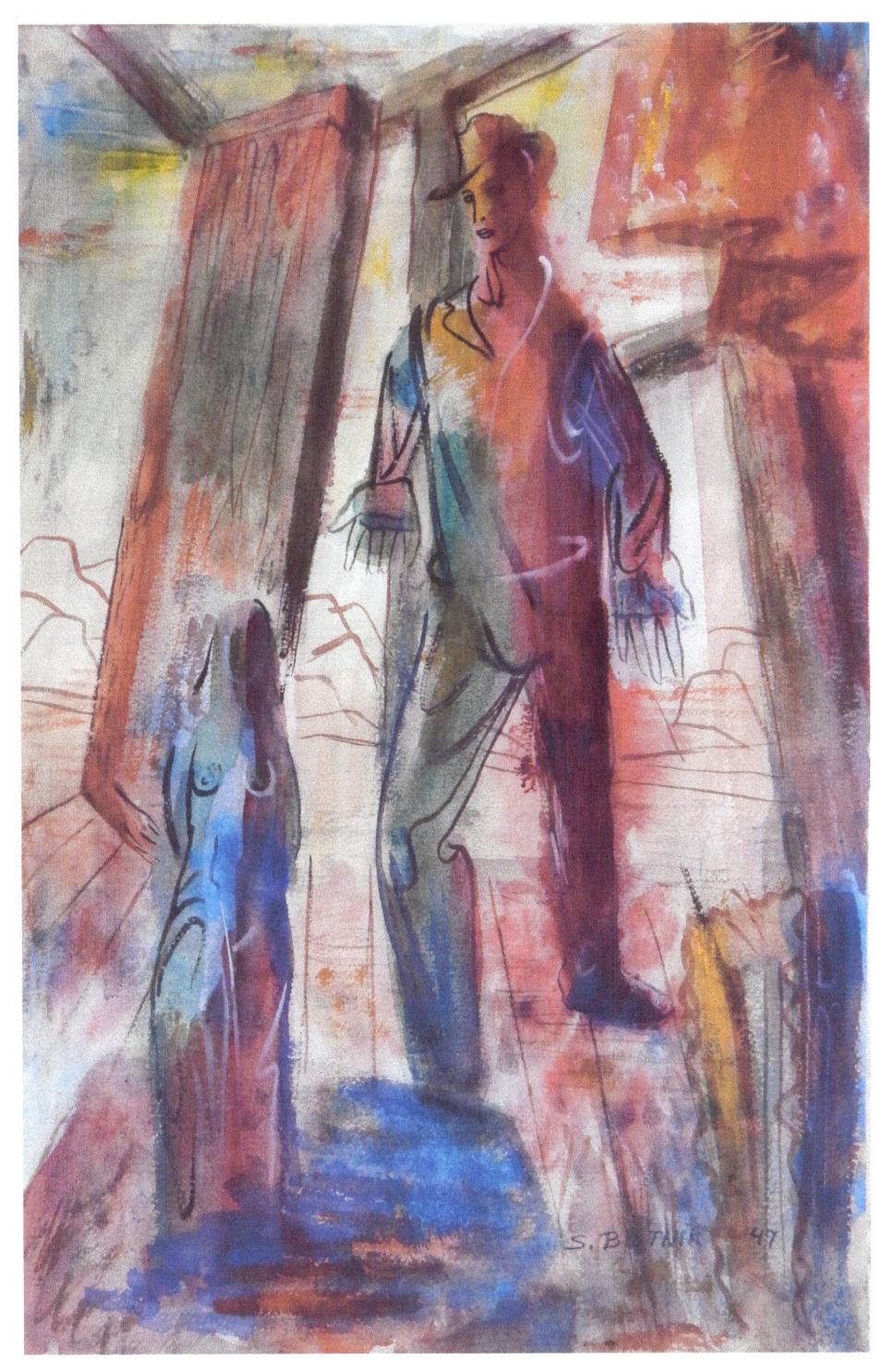

Design and Creation, 1947
Watercolor on paper, 21.75 x 15 in.
ARTneo Collection, Gift of the artist

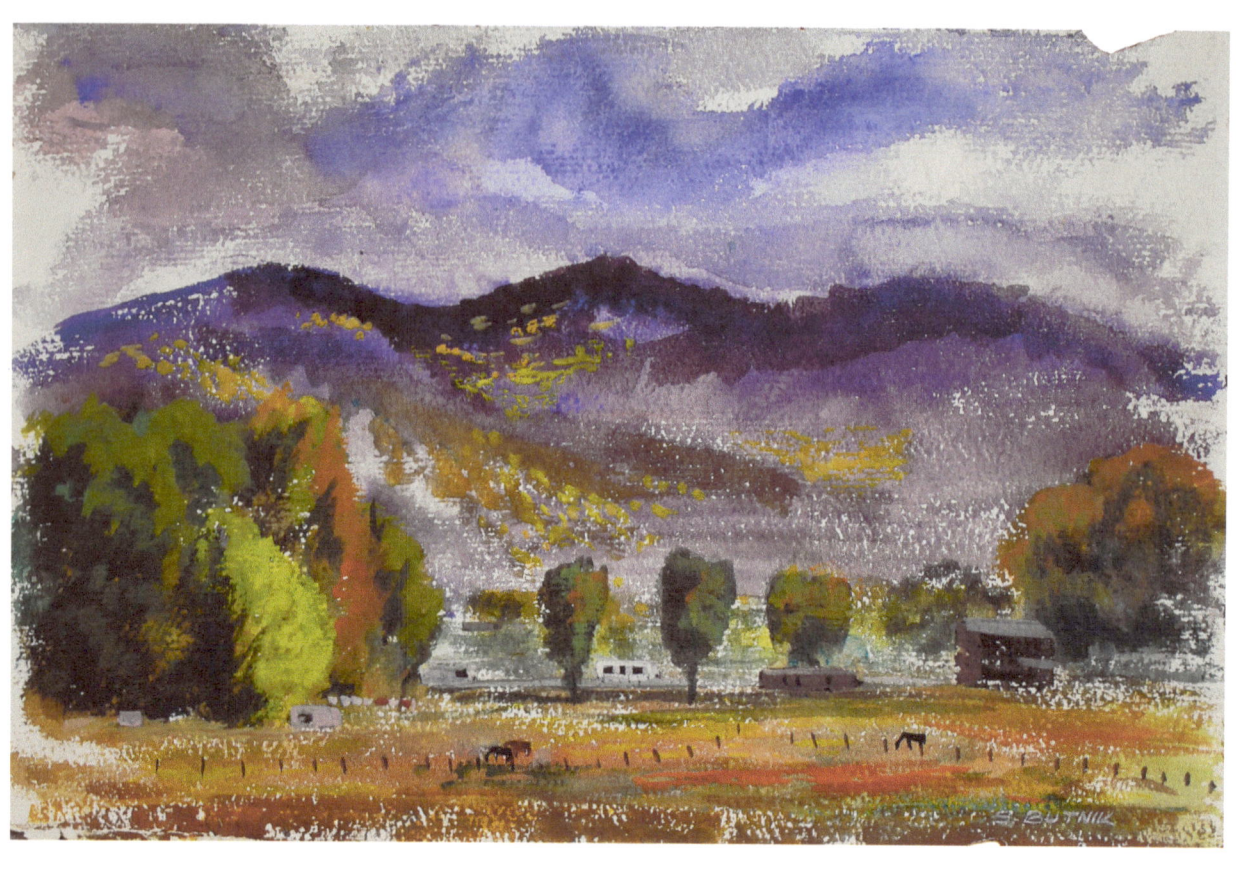

Taos 1947, 1947
Watercolor on paper, 12 x 18 in.
ARTneo Collection, Gift of the artist

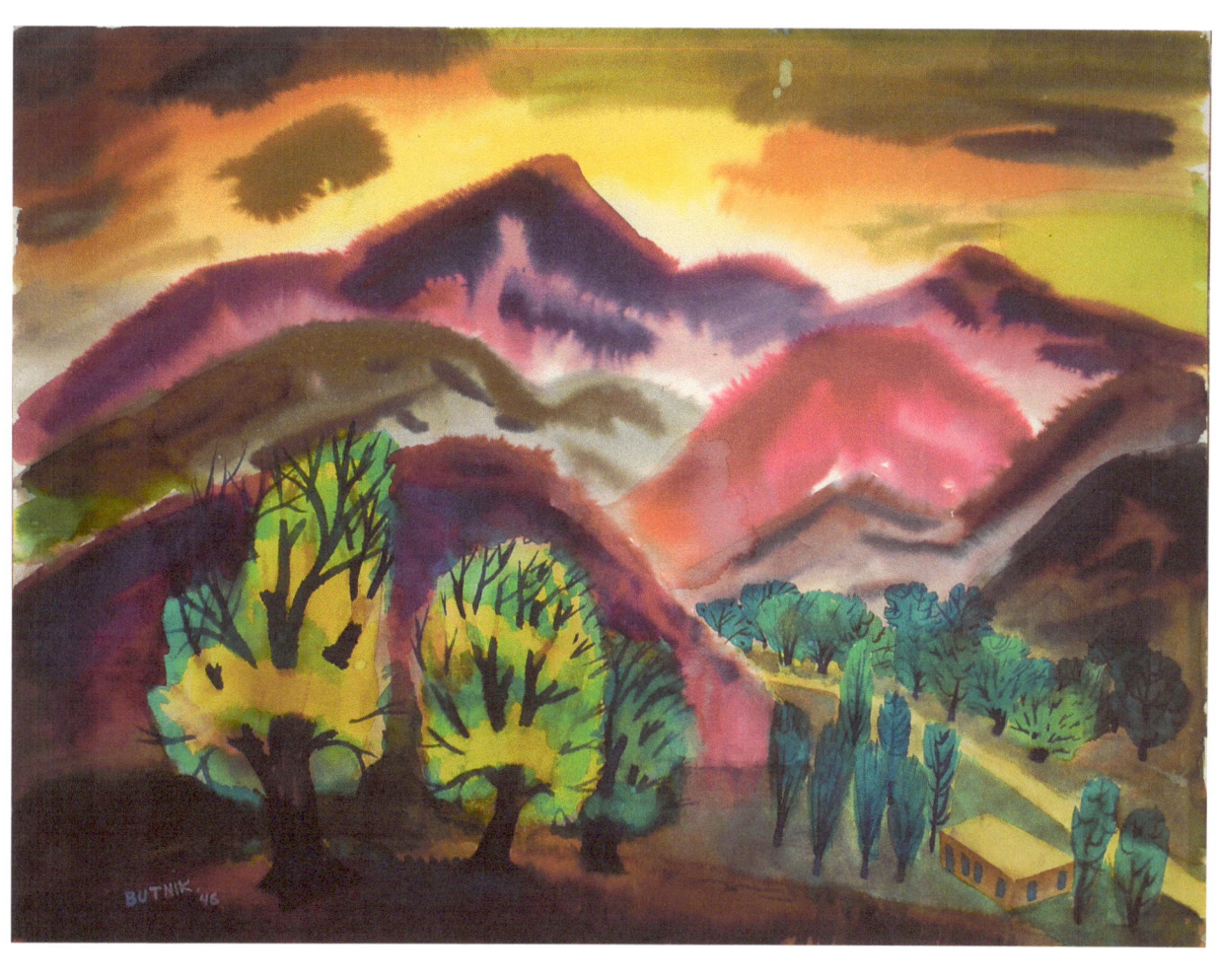

Arroyo, 1948
Watercolor on paper, 15 x 22 in.
ARTneo Collection, Gift of the artist

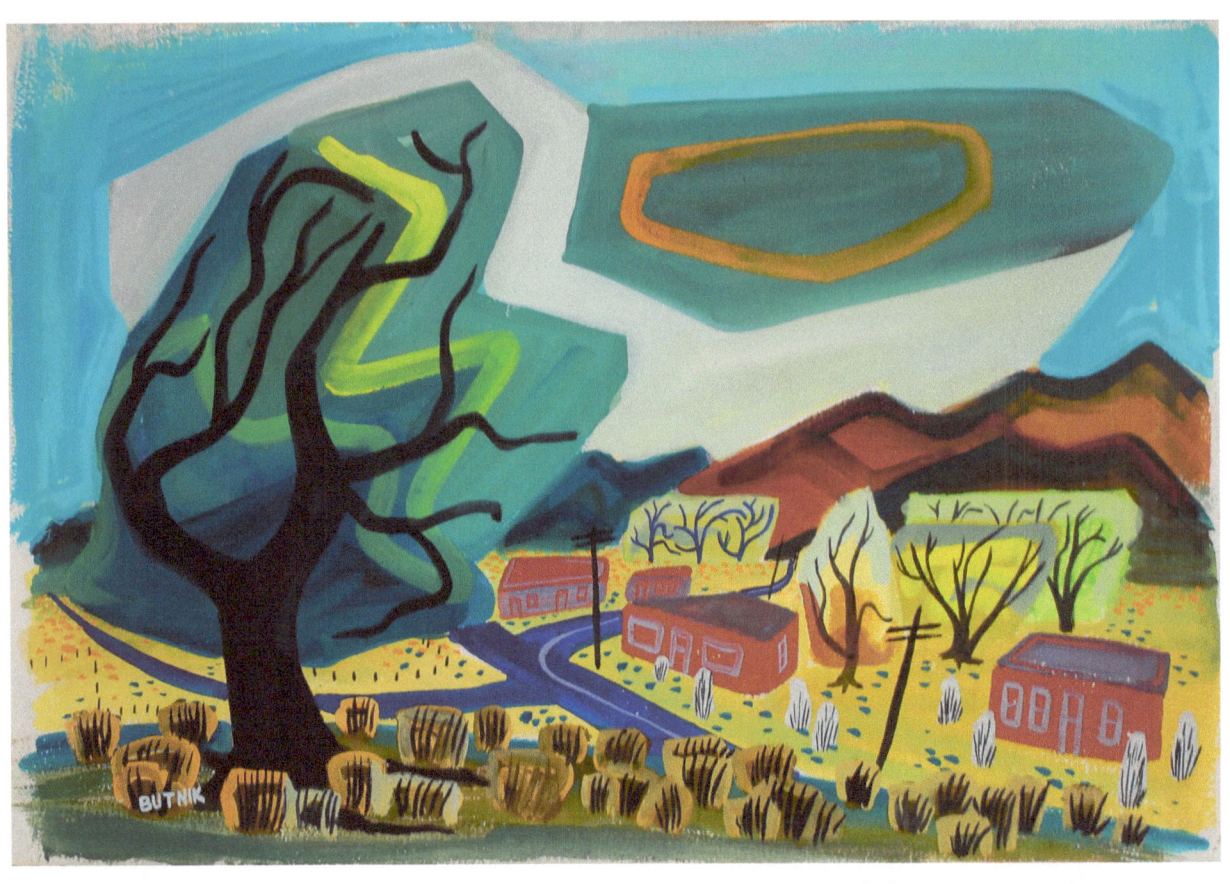

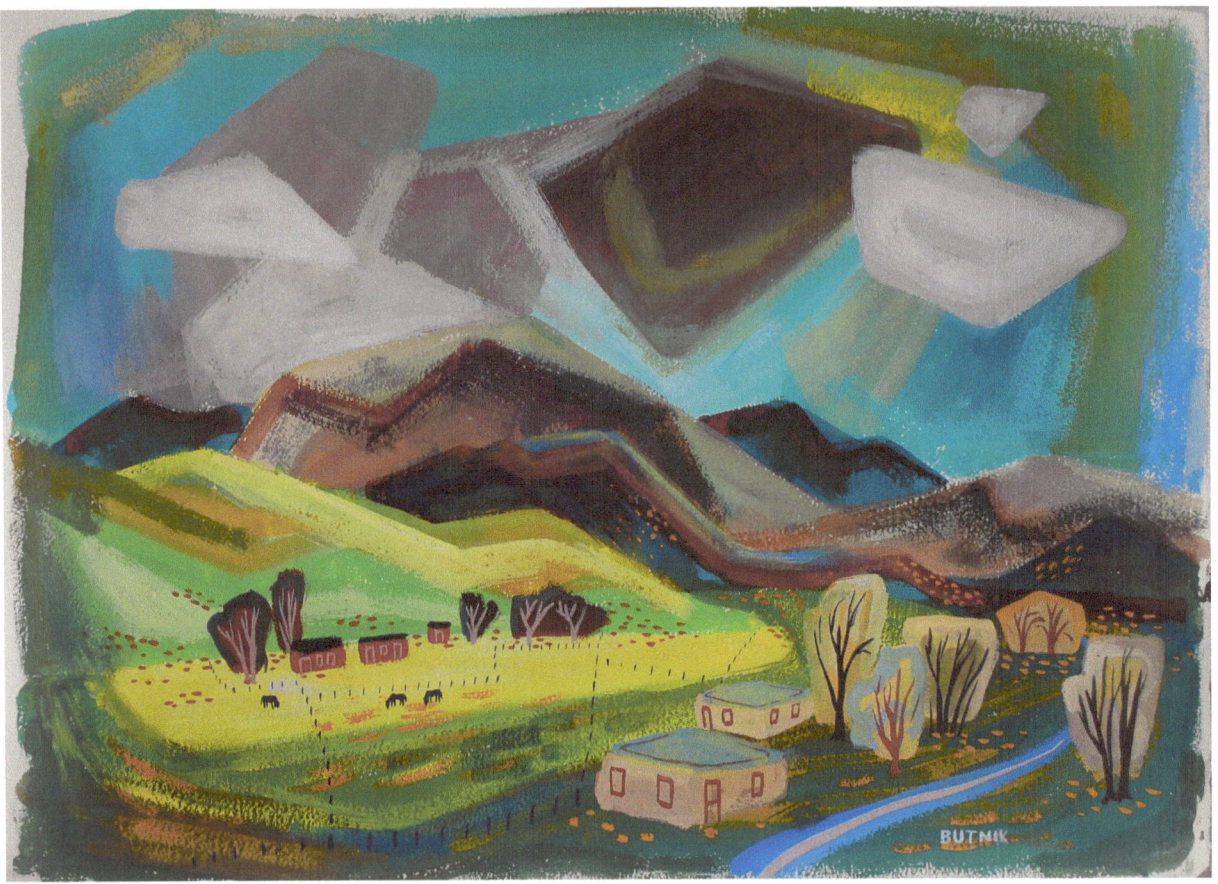

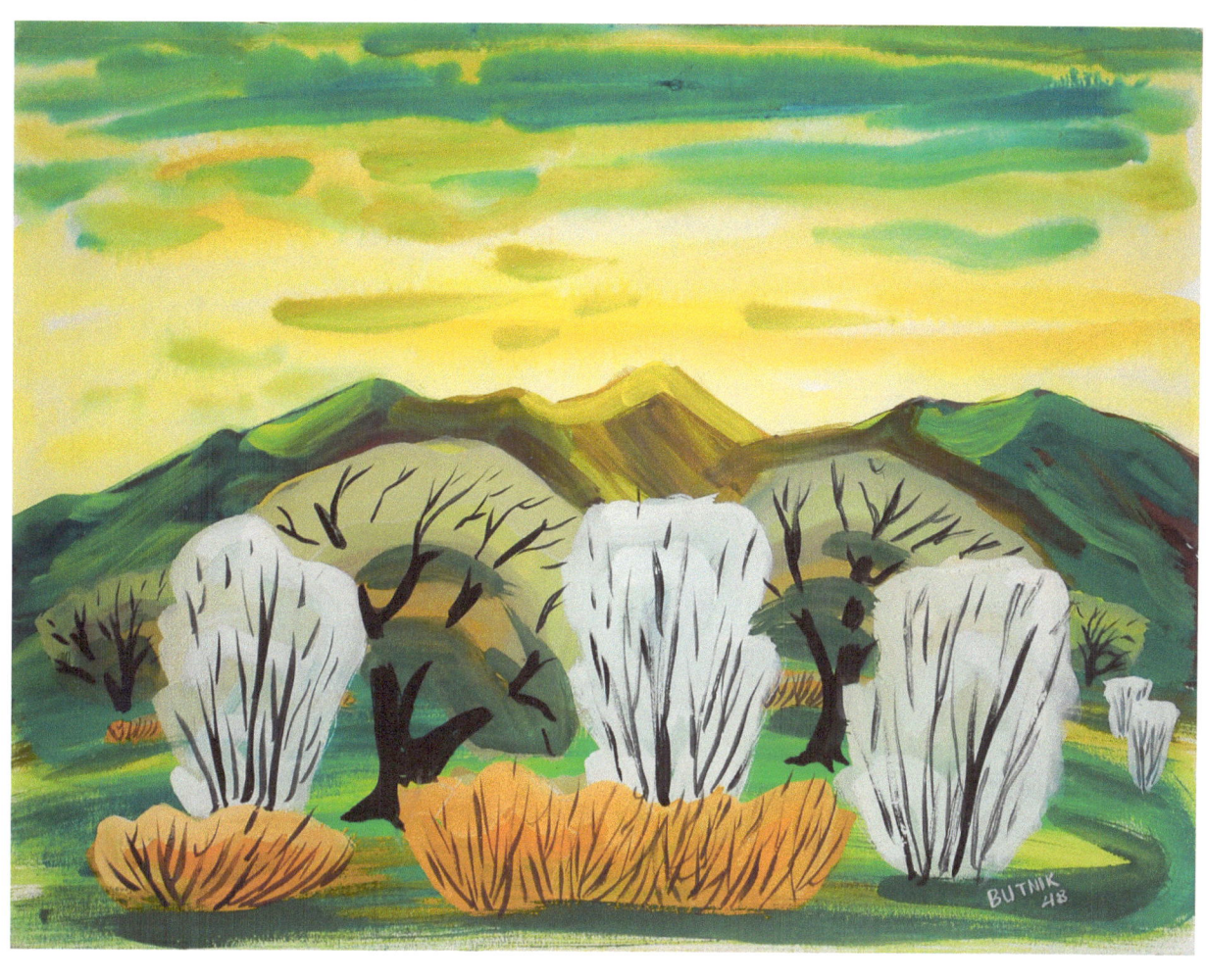

Taos 1948, No. 9, 1948
Watercolor on paper, 11.25 x 15 in.
ARTneo Collection, Gift of the artist

Opposite:
Taos 1948, No. 6, 1948
Watercolor on paper, 15 x 22 in.
ARTneo Collection, Gift of the artist

Valley Road 2, 1948
Casein on paper, 15 x 22 in.
ARTneo Collection, Gift of the artist

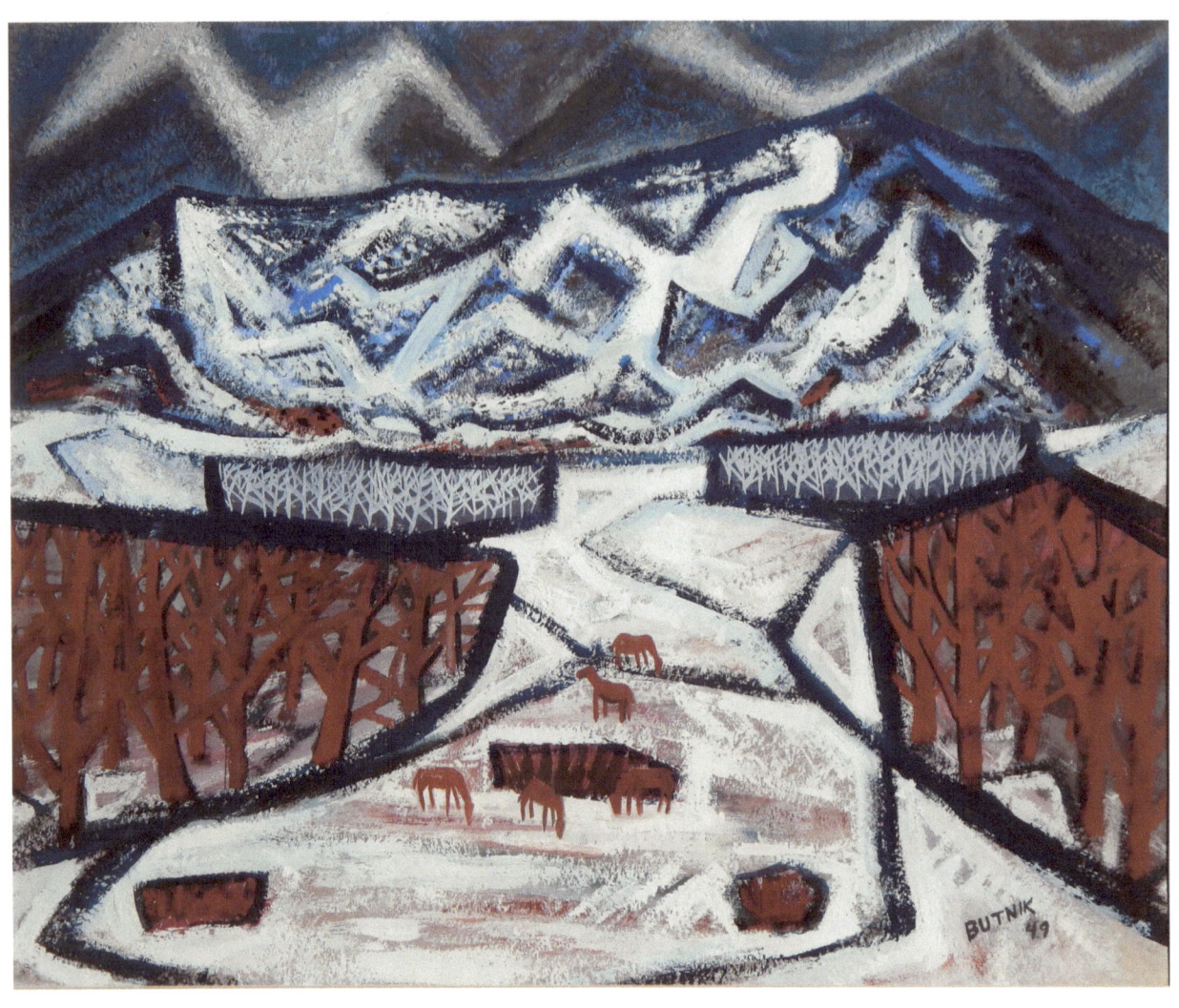

Mid Winter Day, Taos, New Mexico, 1947
Casein on paper, 18 x 23 in.
ARTneo Collection, Gift of the artist

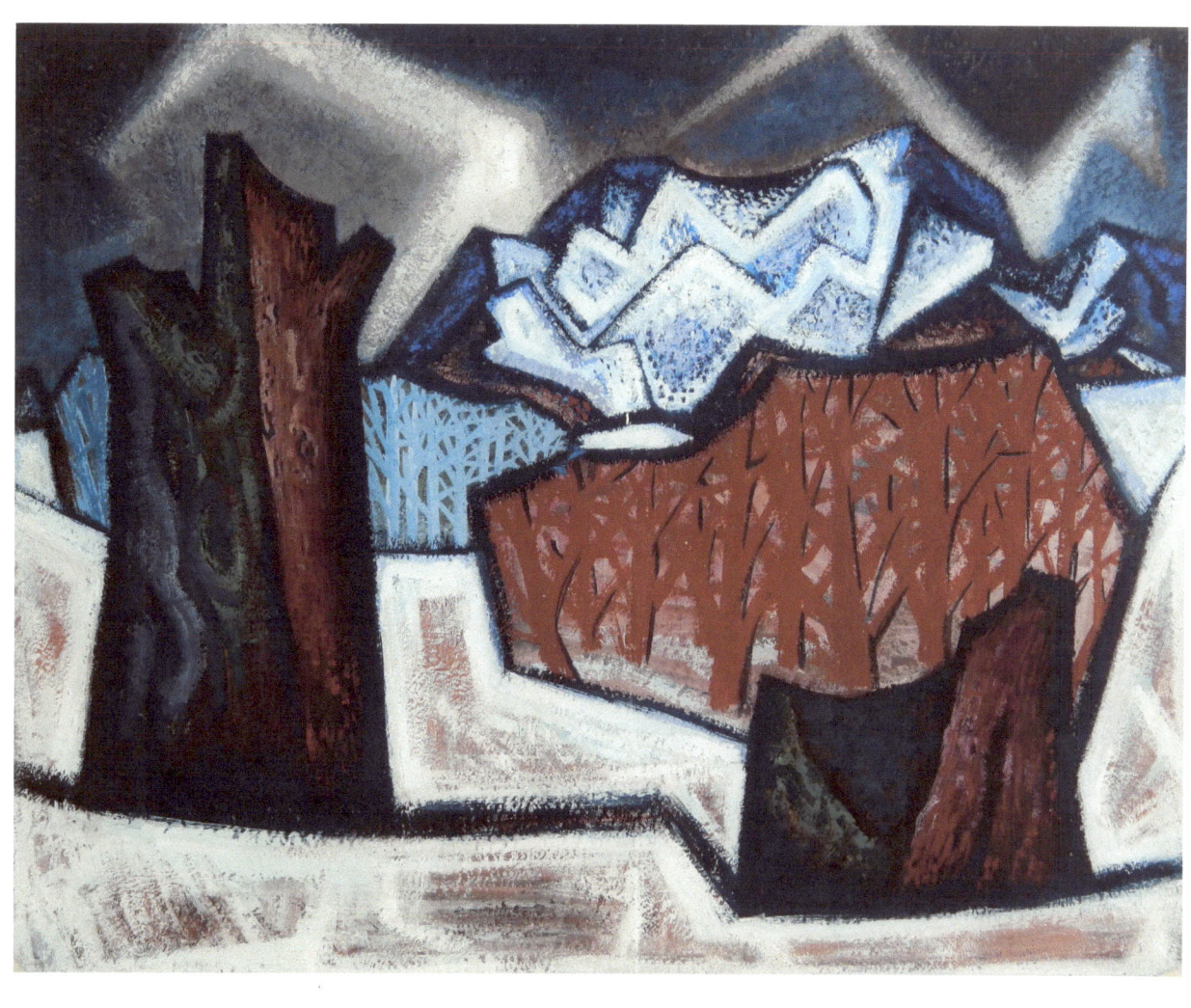

Mid Winter Day, Taos, New Mexico, No. 2, 1947
Casein on paper, 19 x 23.25 in.
ARTneo Collection, Gift of the artist

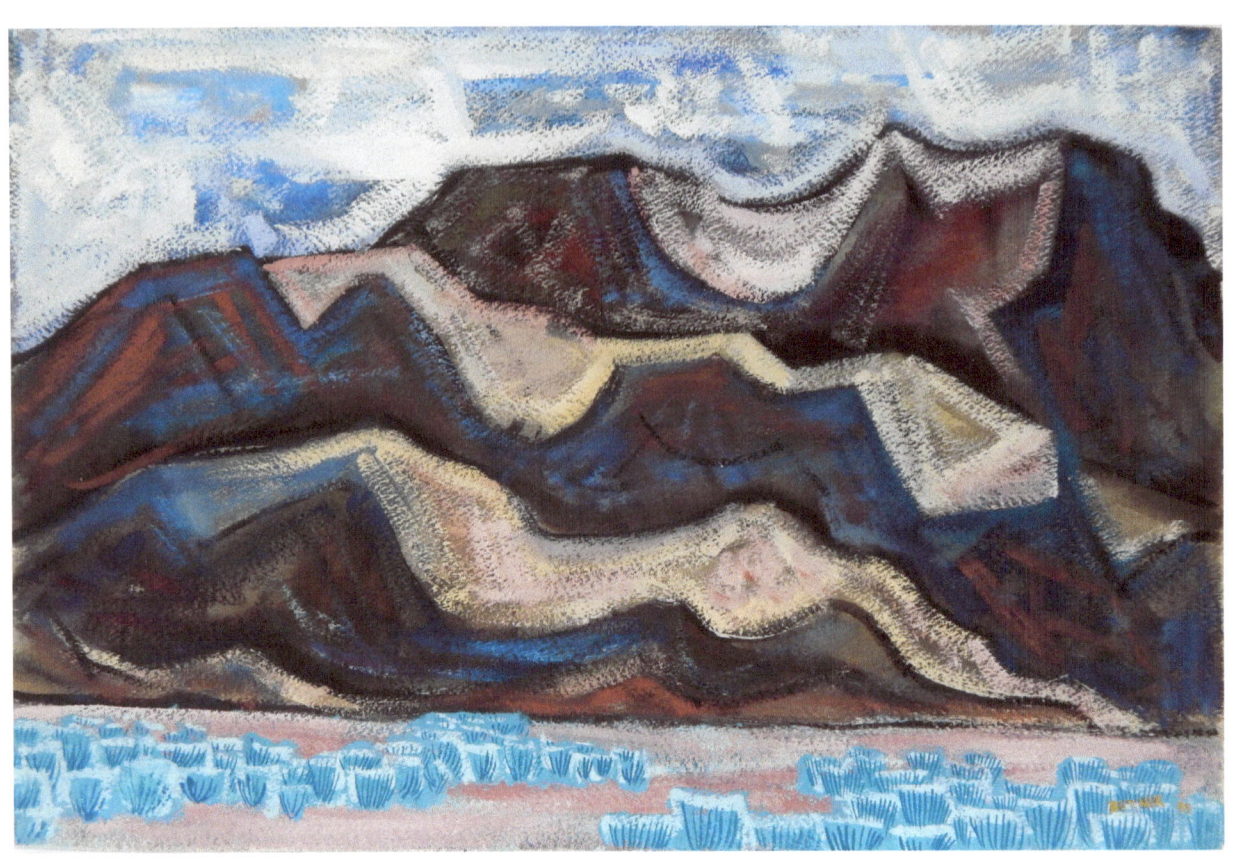

The Hills Beyond, 1948
Casein on paper, 13.5 x 21.5 in.
ARTneo Collection, Gift of the artist

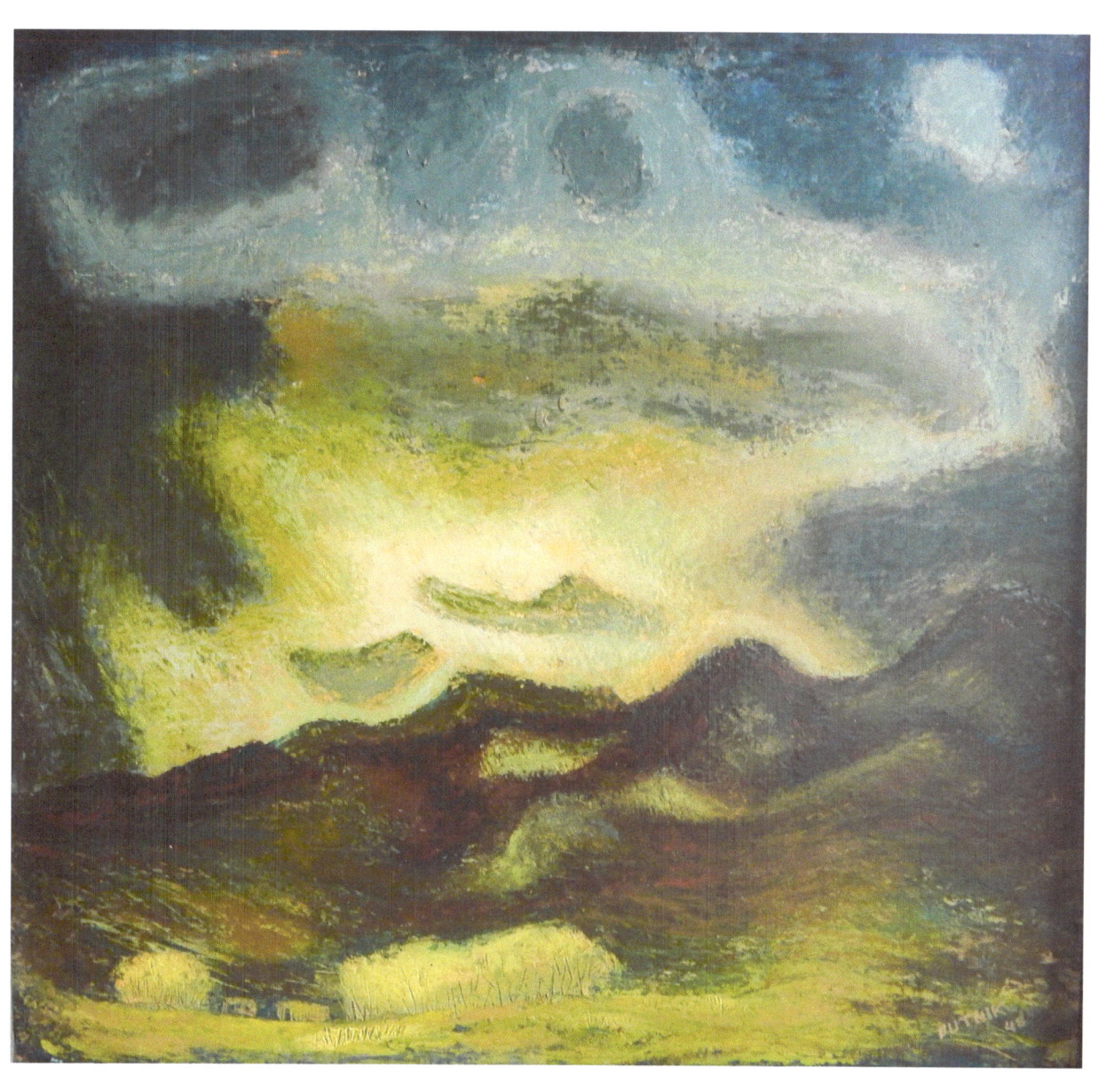

Taos Vista, 1948
Acrylic on board, 24 x 26 in.
ARTneo Collection, Gift of the artist

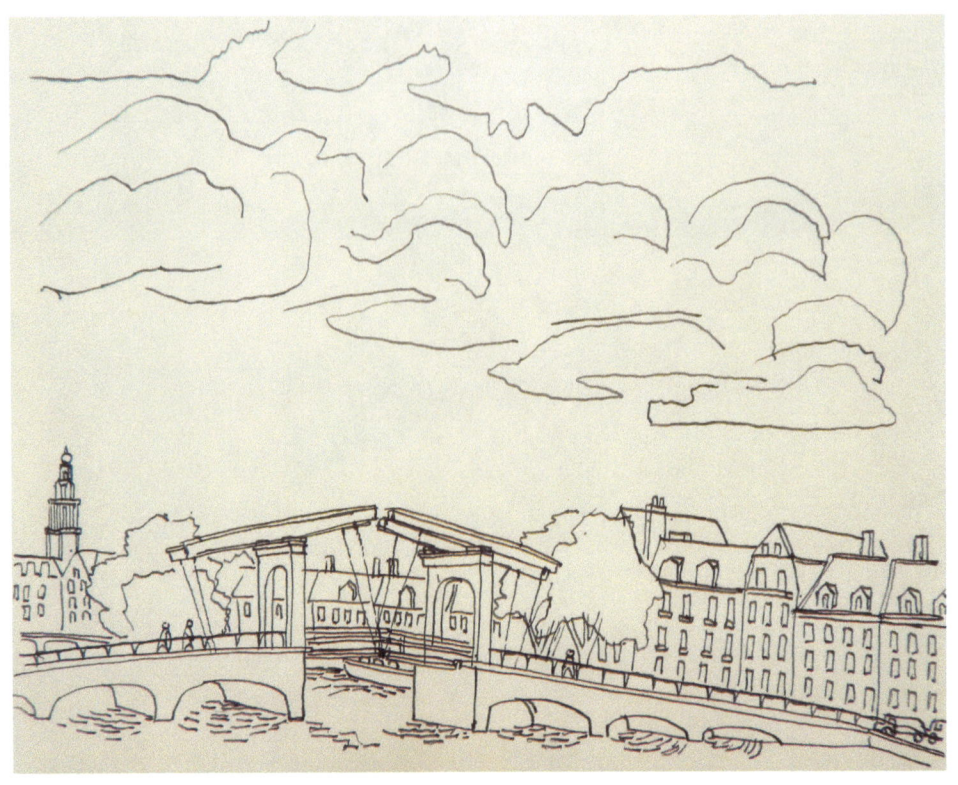

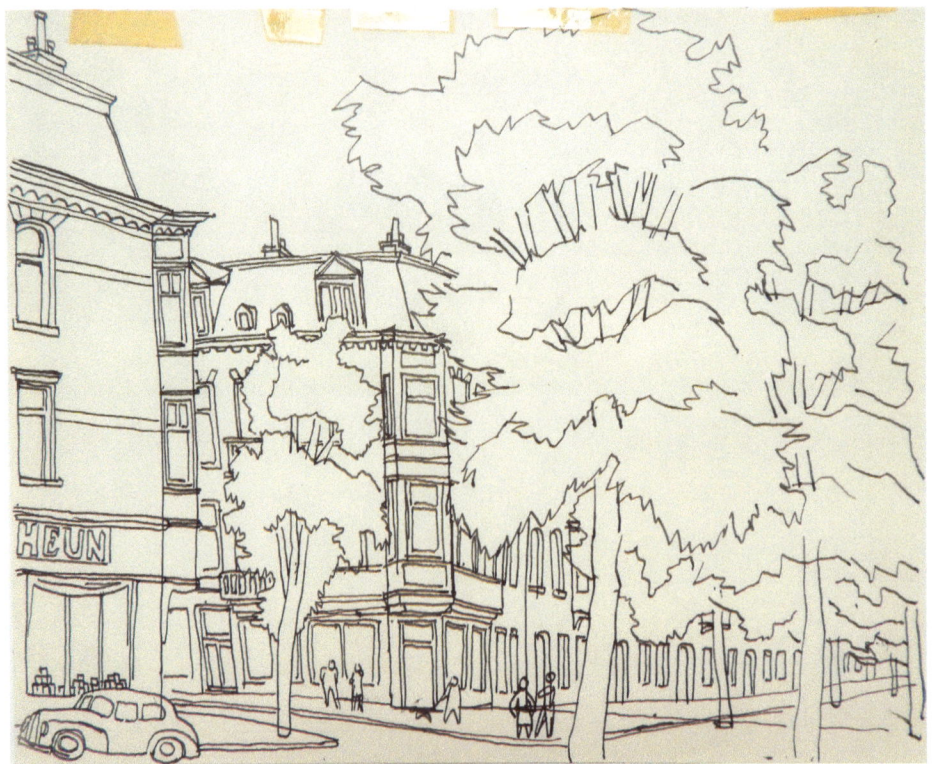

Amsterdam, Holland, 1955
Ink on paper, 7.5 x 9.5 in.
ARTneo Collection, Gift of the artist

Amsterdam, Holland, 1955
Ink on paper, 7.5 x 9.5 in.
ARTneo Collection, Gift of the artist

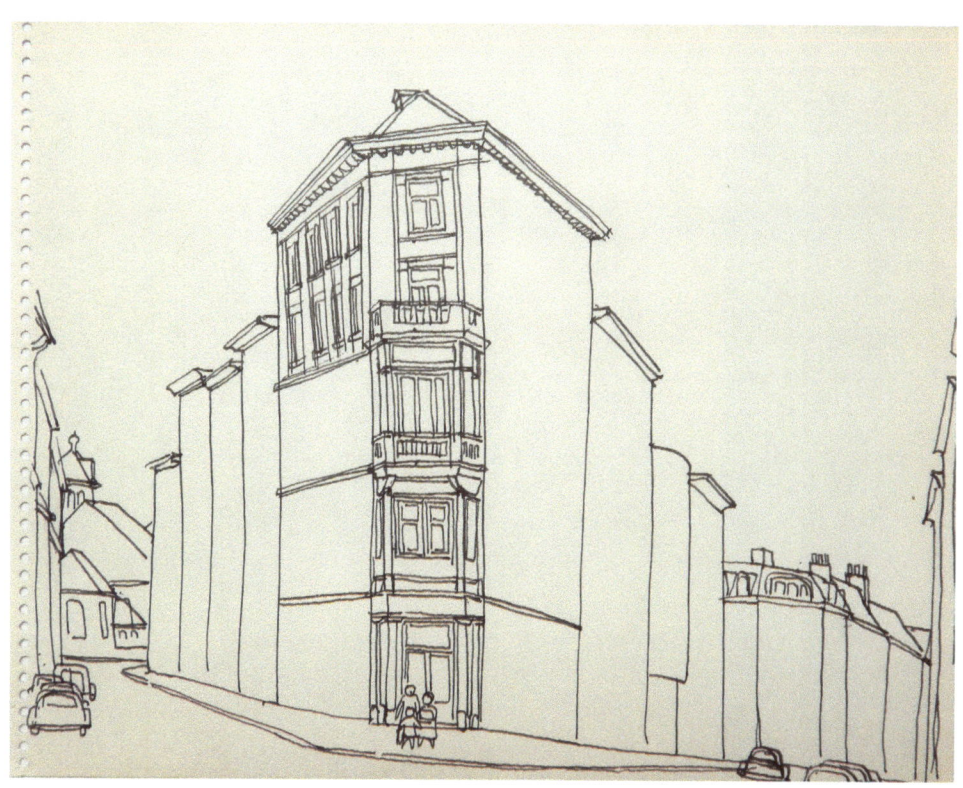

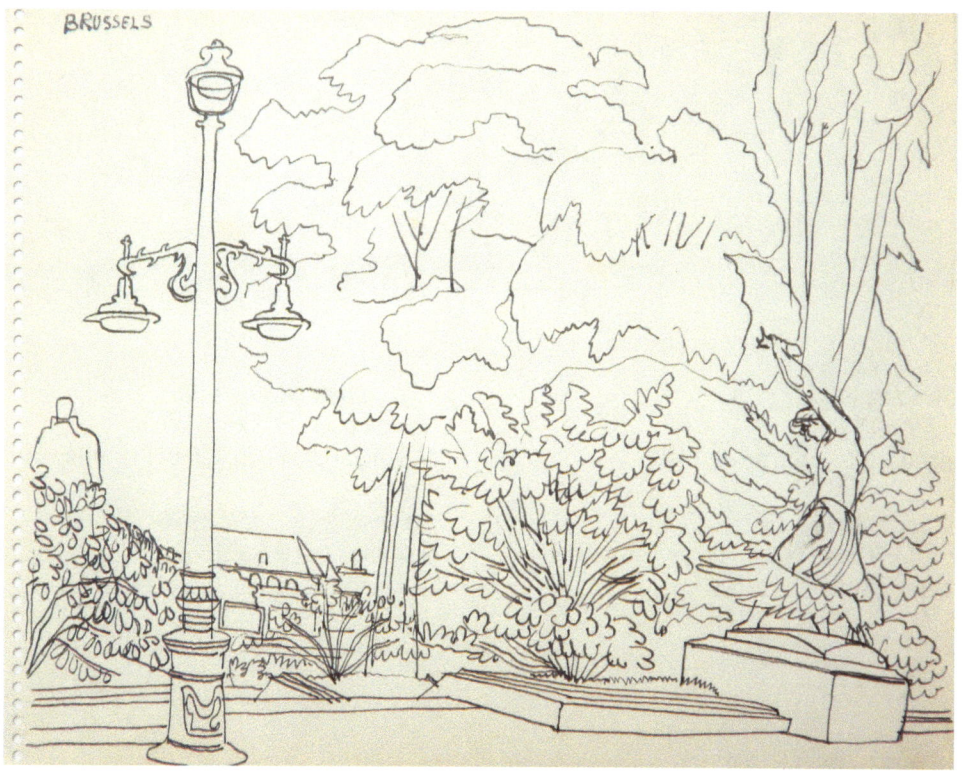

Brussels, Belgium, 1955
Ink on paper, 7.5 x 9.5 in.
ARTneo Collection, Gift of the artist

Brussels, Belgium, 1955
Ink on paper, 7.5 x 9.5 in.
ARTneo Collection, Gift of the artist

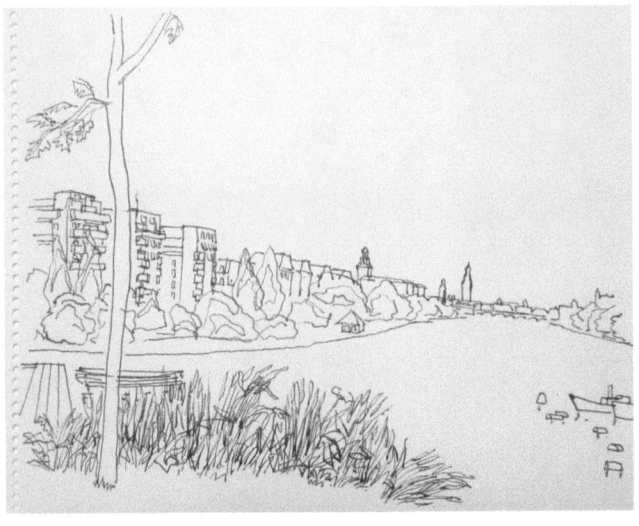

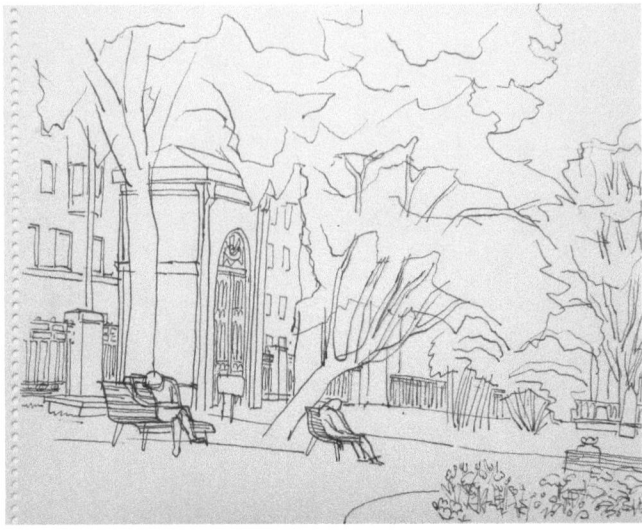

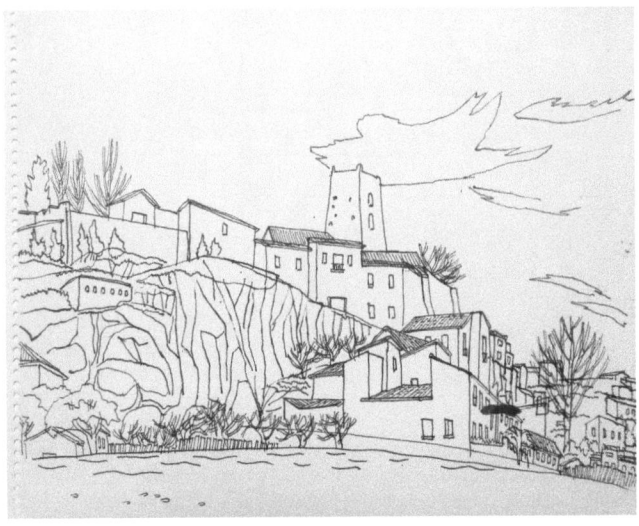

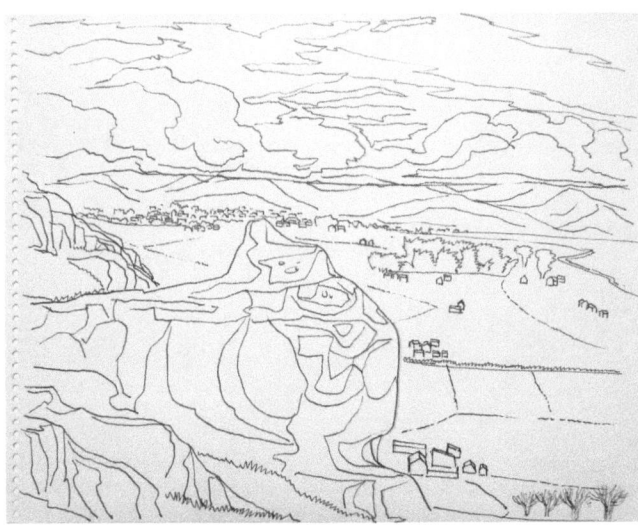

Stockholm, Sweden, 1955
Ink on paper, 7.5 x 9.5 in.
ARTneo Collection, Gift of the artist

Torremolinos, Spain, 1956
Ink on paper, 7.5 x 9.5 in.
ARTneo Collection, Gift of the artist

Stockholm, Sweden, 1955
Ink on paper, 7.5 x 9.5 in.
ARTneo Collection, Gift of the artist

Torremolinos, Spain, 1956
Ink on paper, 7.5 x 9.5 in.
ARTneo Collection, Gift of the artist

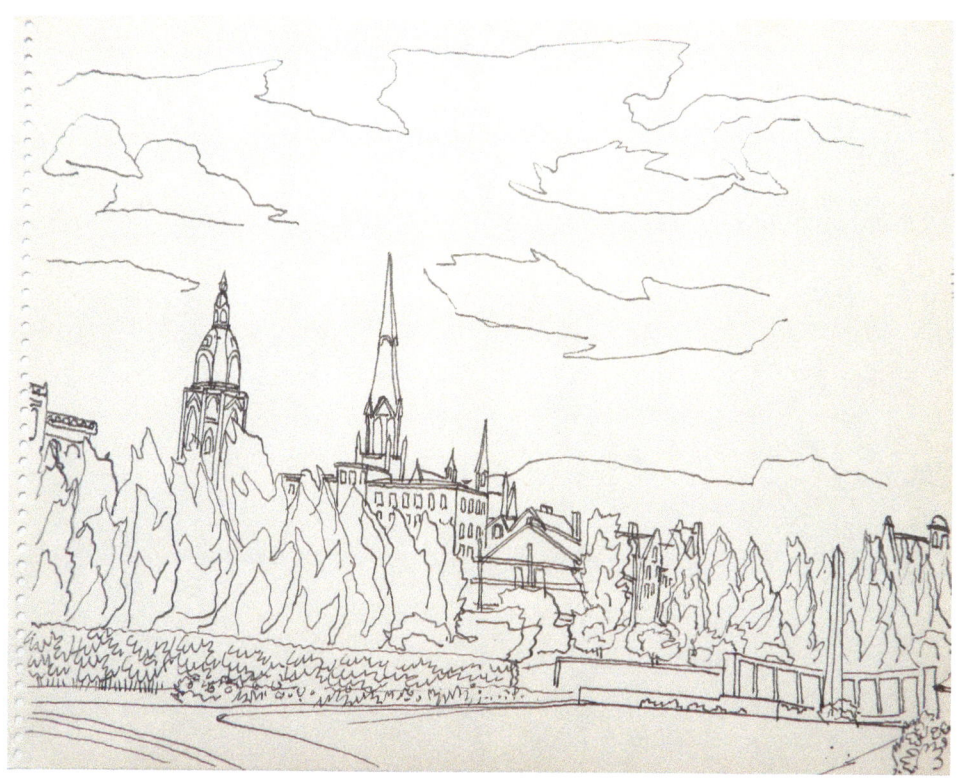

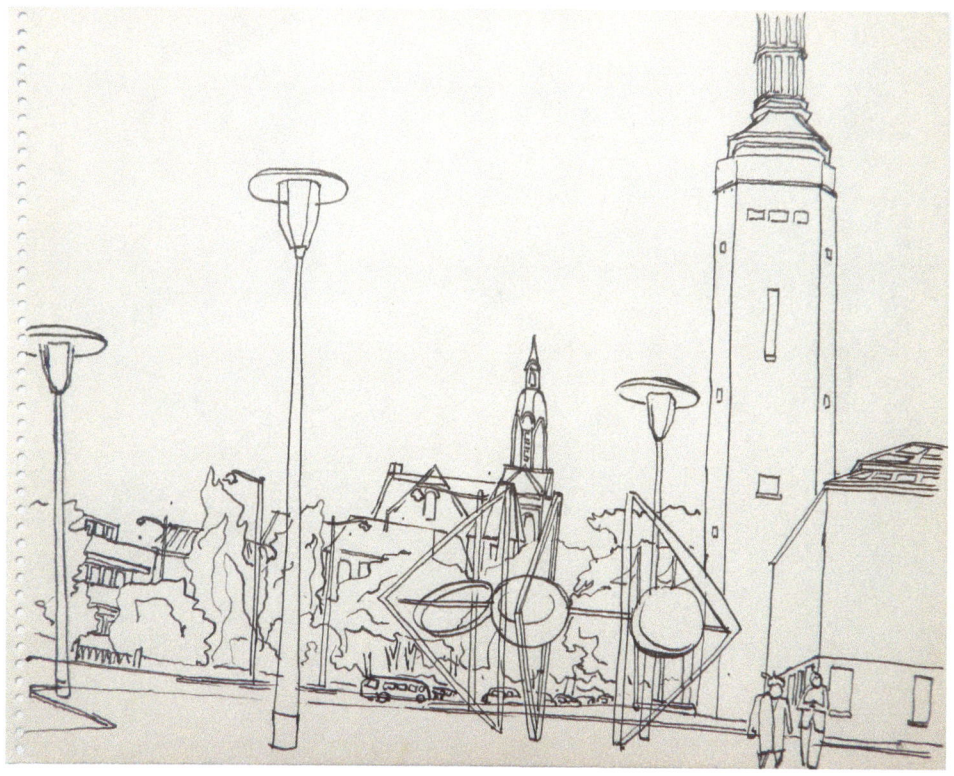

Copenhagen, Denmark, 1955
Ink on paper, 7.5 x 9.5 in.
ARTneo Collection, Gift of the artist

Copenhagen, Denmark, 1955
Ink on paper, 7.5 x 9.5 in.
ARTneo Collection, Gift of the artist

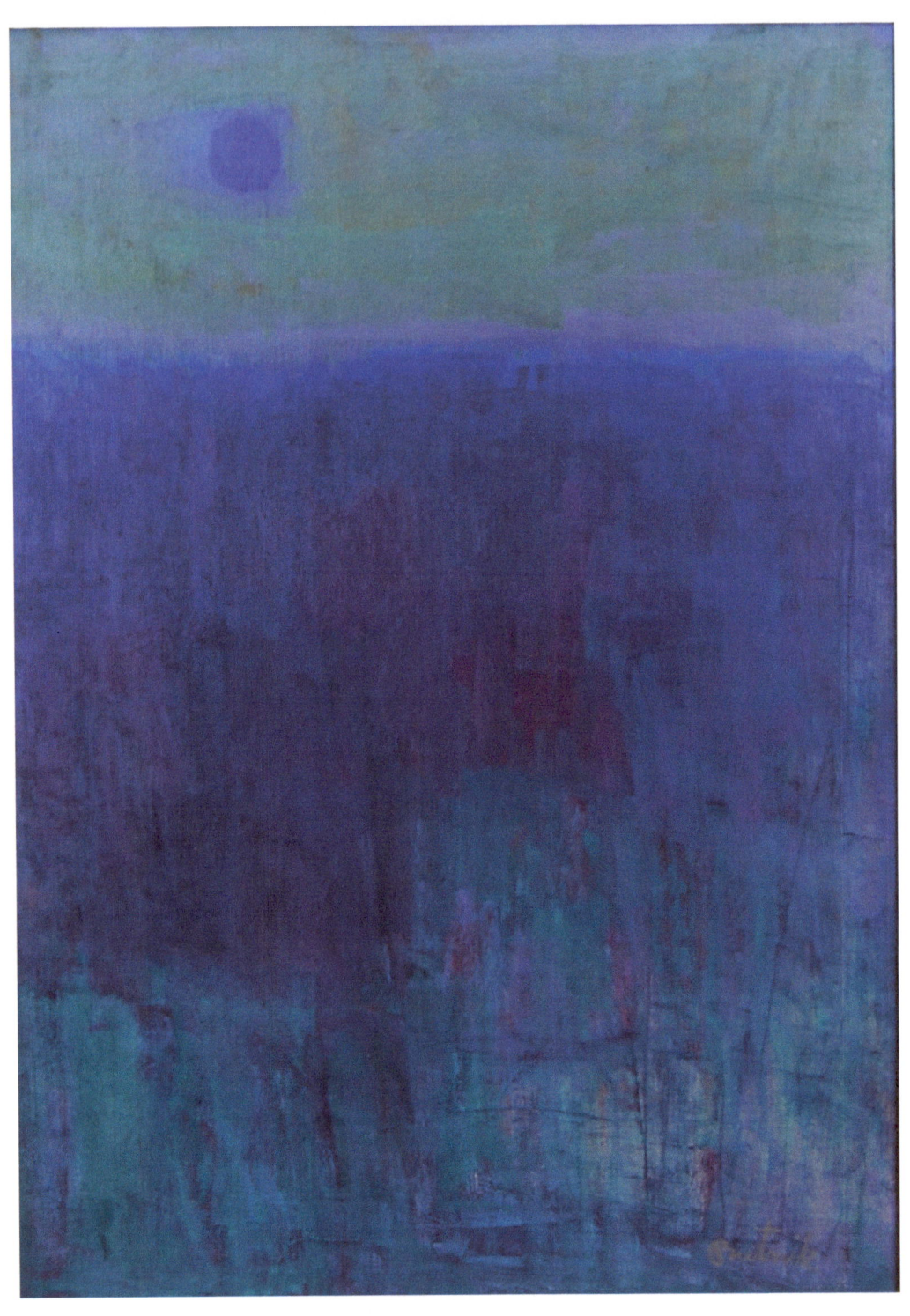

Back of the Moon, # 2, 1963
Oil on linen, 30 x 22 in.
Artists Archives of the Western Reserve

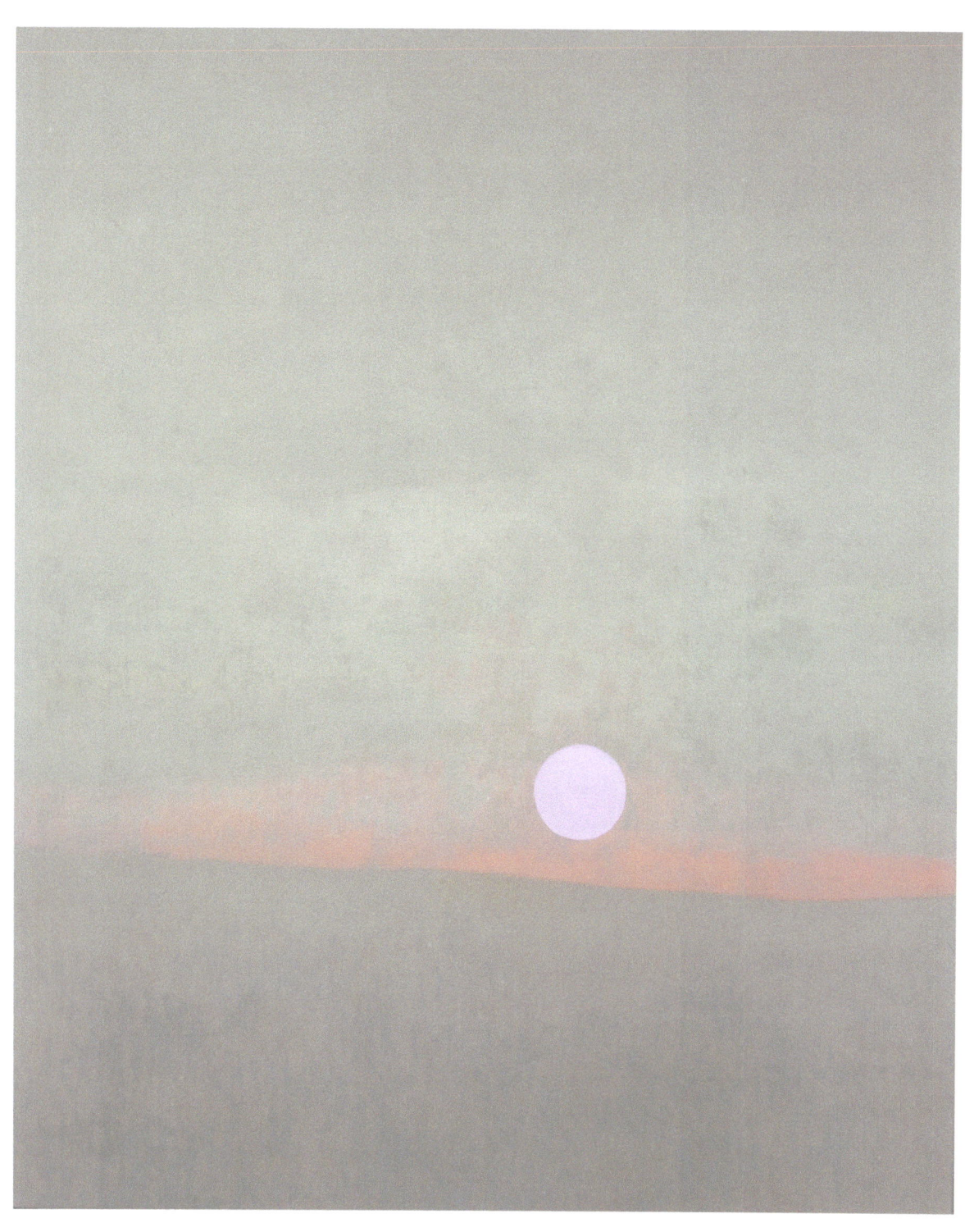

Earth, Sky, Sun, Vista 6, 1972
Acrylic on canvas, 52 x 43 in.
ARTneo Collection, Gift of the artist

Earth, Sky, Sun, Vista 8, 1972
Acrylic on canvas, 48 x 42 in.
ARTneo Collection, Gift of the artist

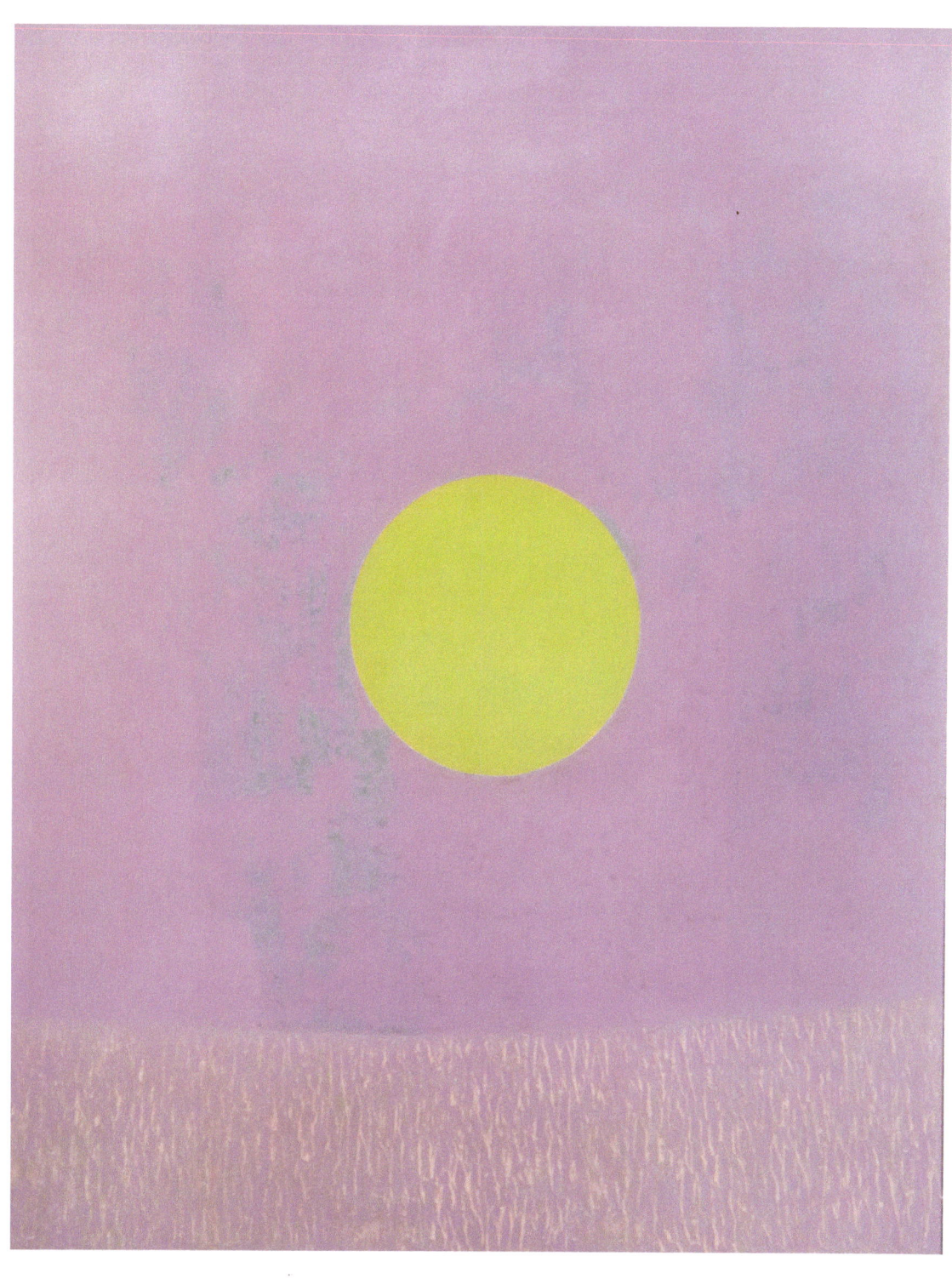

Earth, Sky, Moon, Vista 4, 1972
Acrylic on canvas, 64 x 51 in.
ARTneo Collection, Gift of the artist

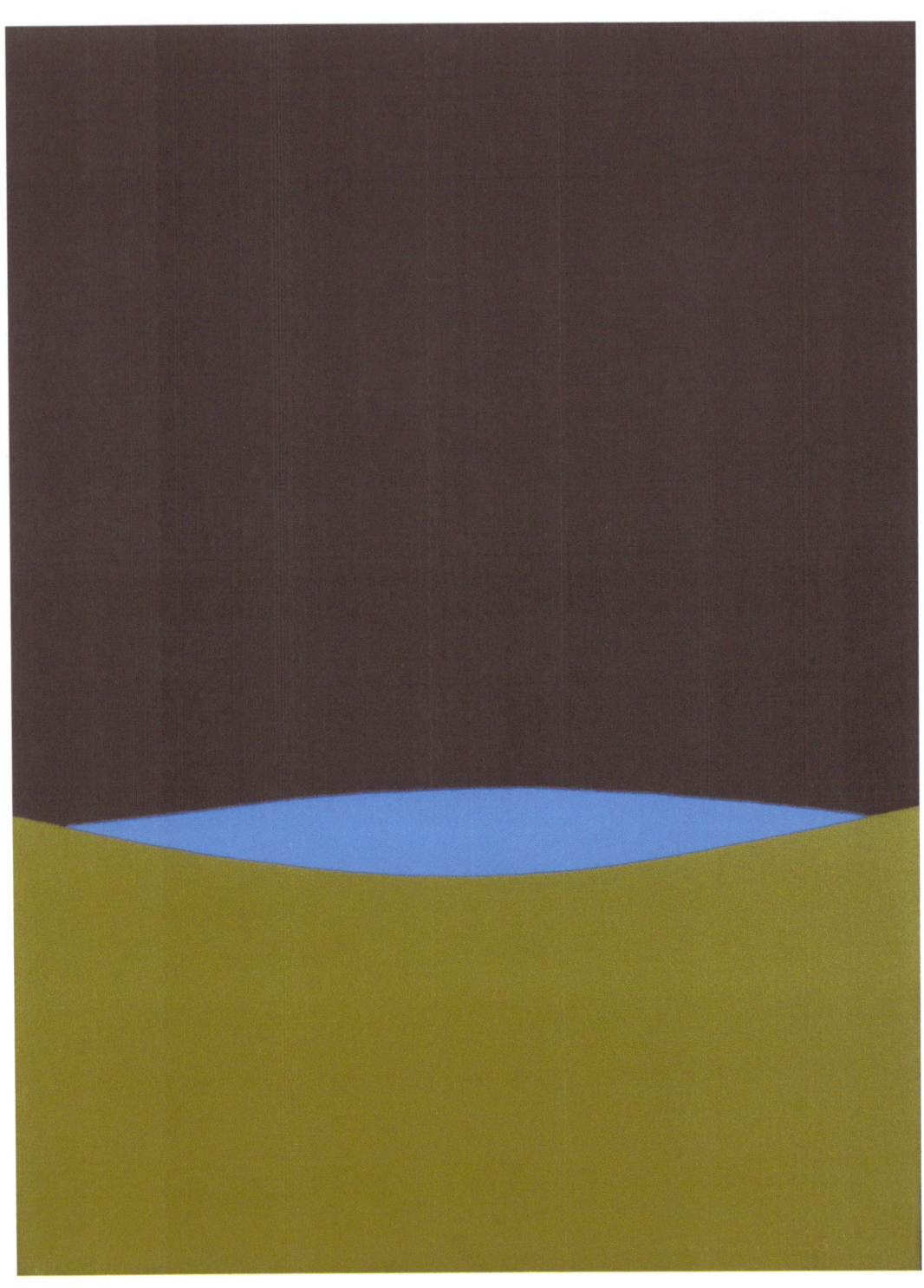

The Sky Beyond #6, 1969
Acrylic on canvas, 36 x 27 in.
Artists Archives of the Western Reserve

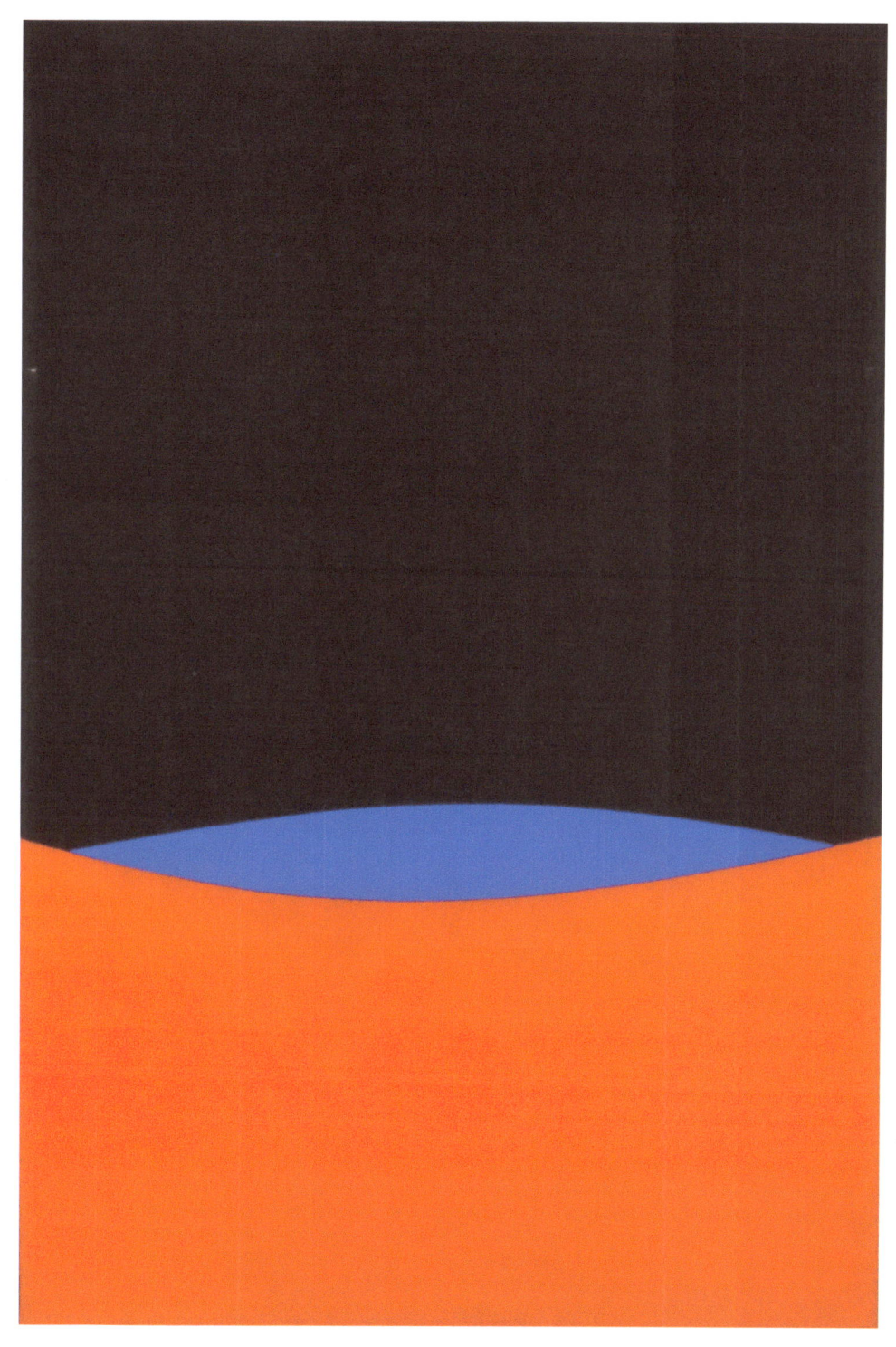

The Sky Beyond #44, 1969
Acrylic on canvas, 47.25 x 28 in.
Artists Archives of the Western Reserve

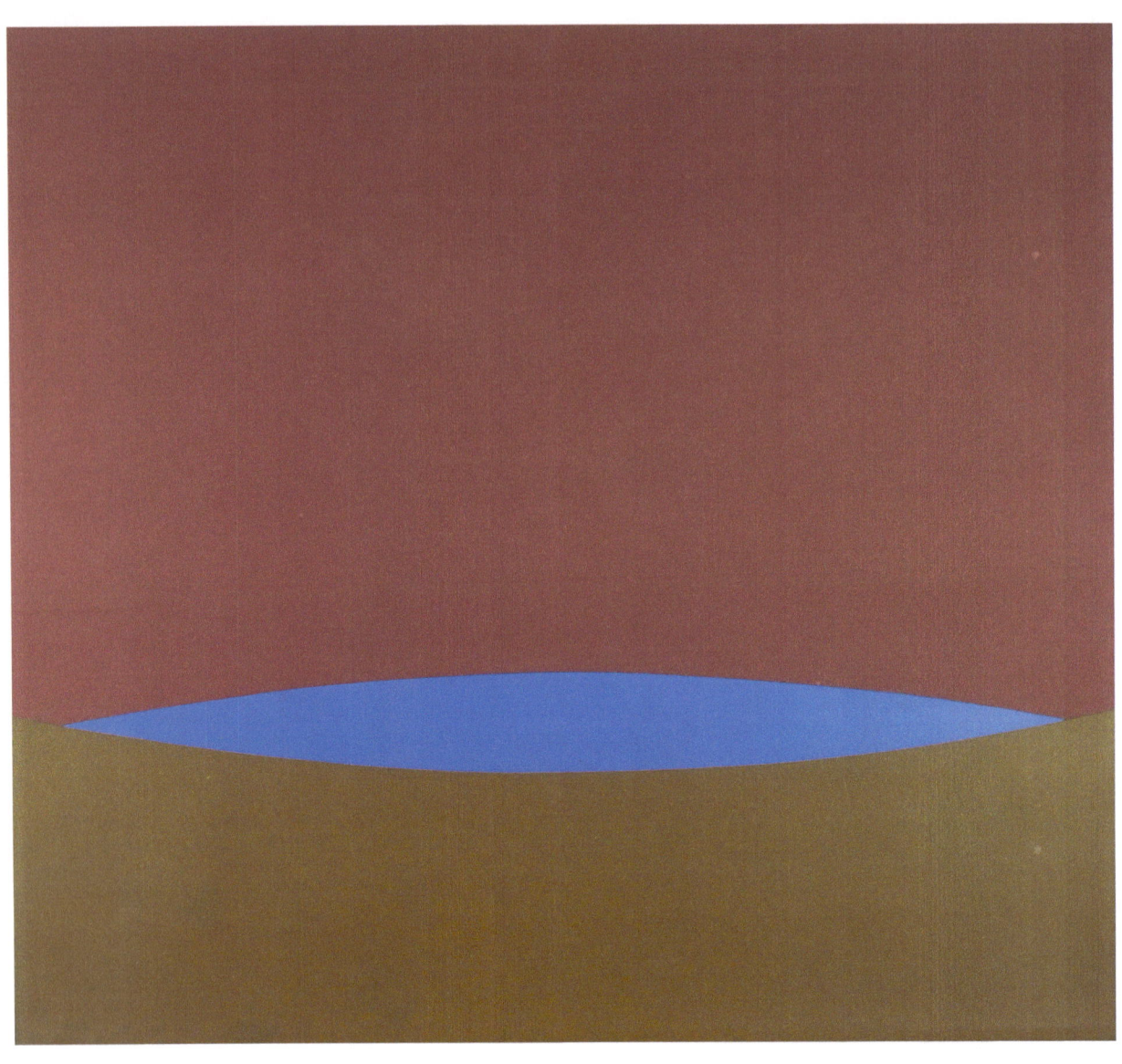

The Sky Beyond #29, 1971
Acrylic on canvas, 48 x 54 in.
Artists Archives of the Western Reserve

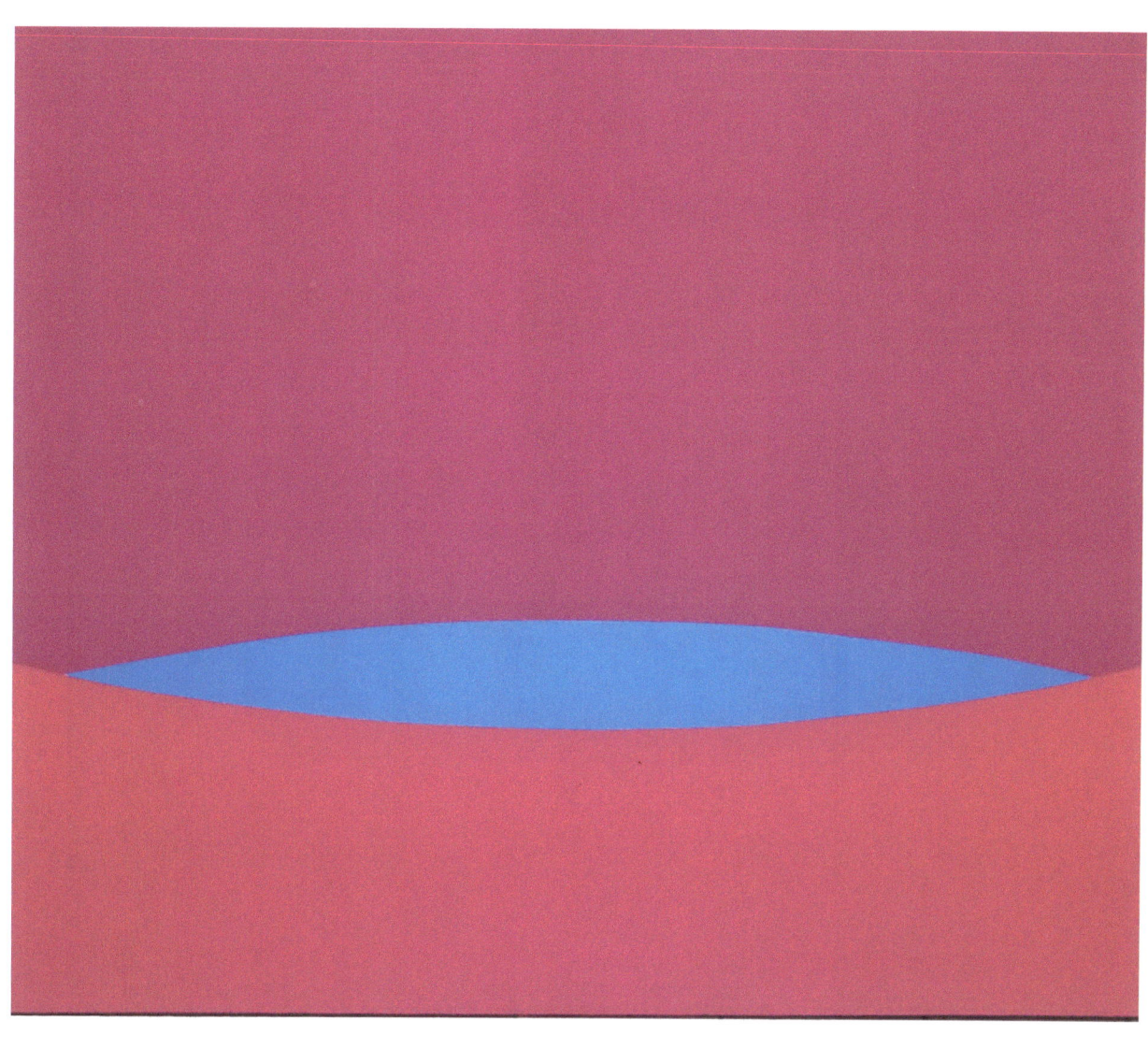

The Sky Beyond #31, 1972
Acrylic on canvas, 55 x 66 in.
Artists Archives of the Western Reserve

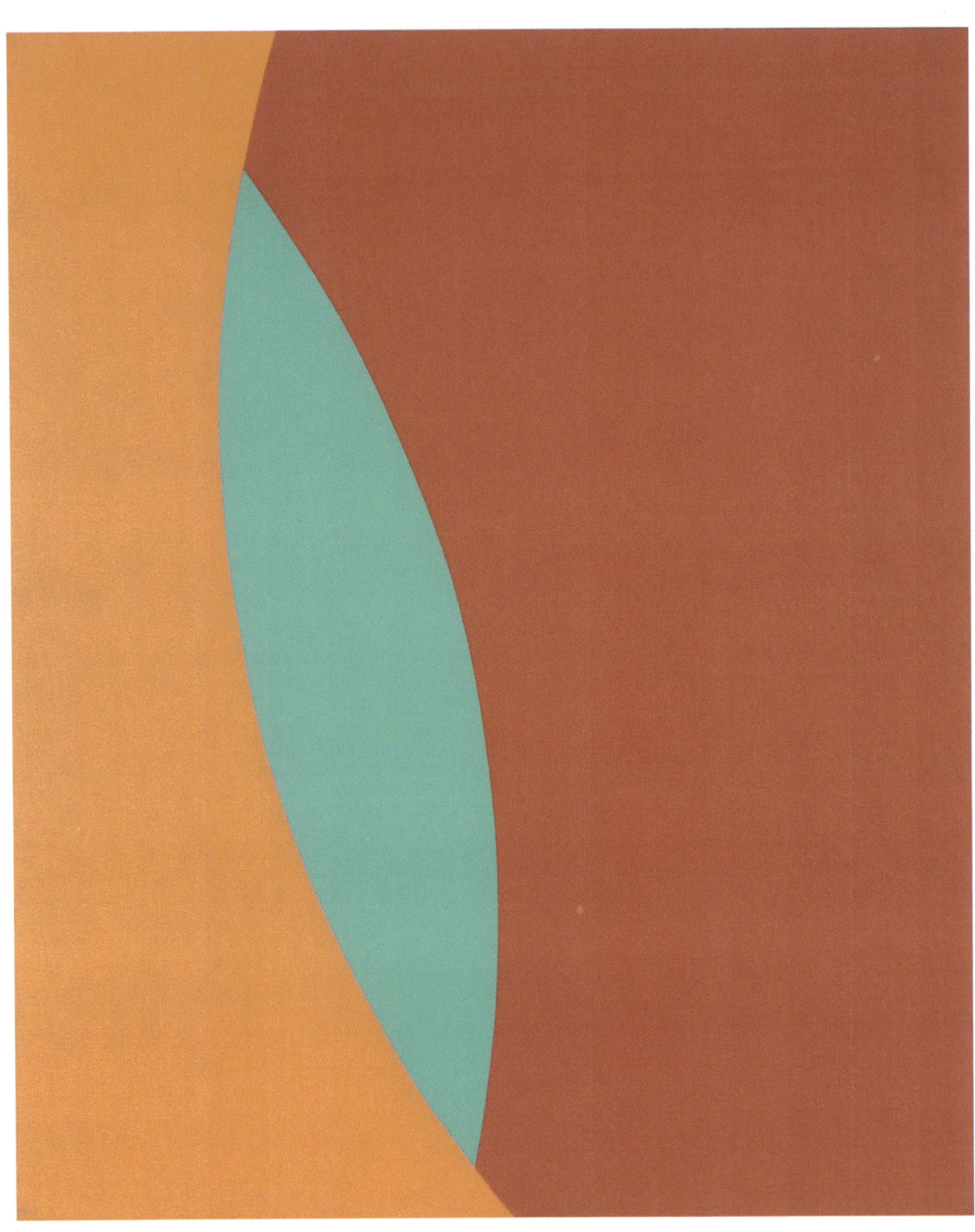

The Sky Beyond #36, 1981
Acrylic on canvas, 50 x 42 in.
Artists Archives of the Western Reserve

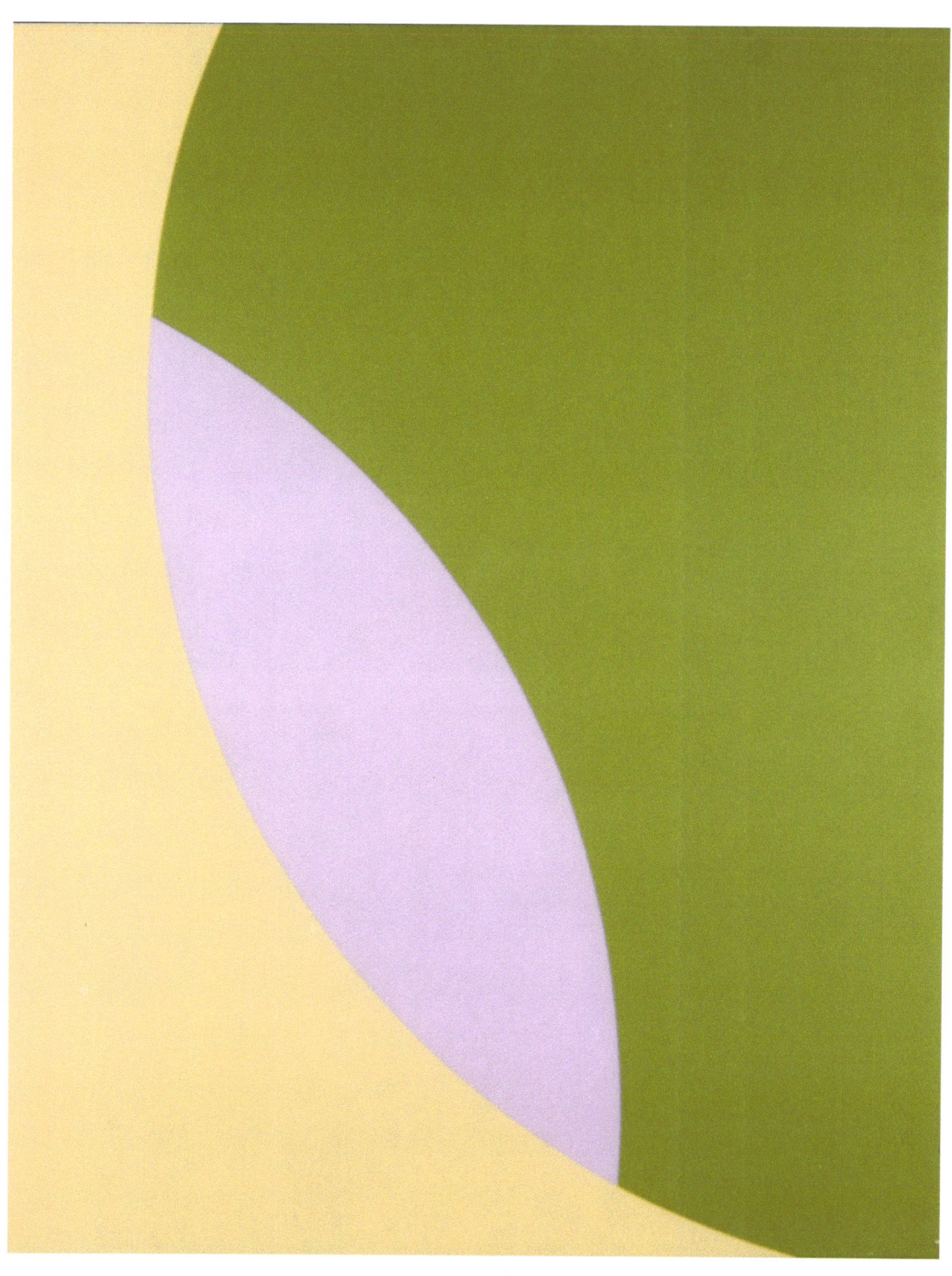

The Sky Beyond #37, 1982
Acrylic on canvas, 48 x 38 in.
Artists Archives of the Western Reserve

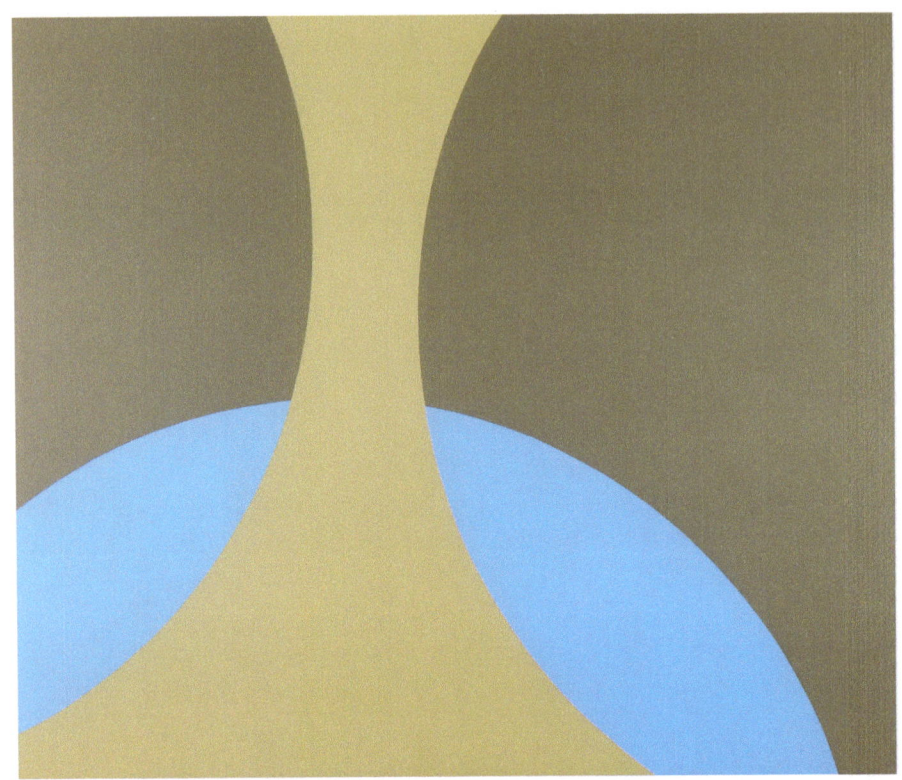

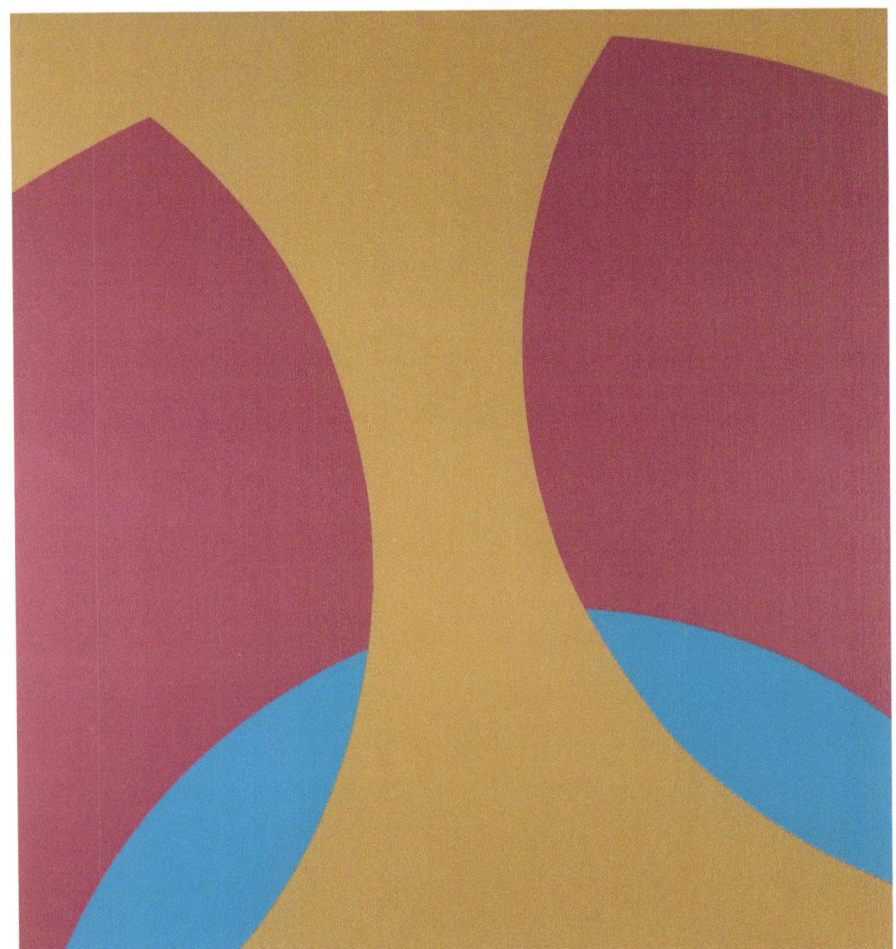

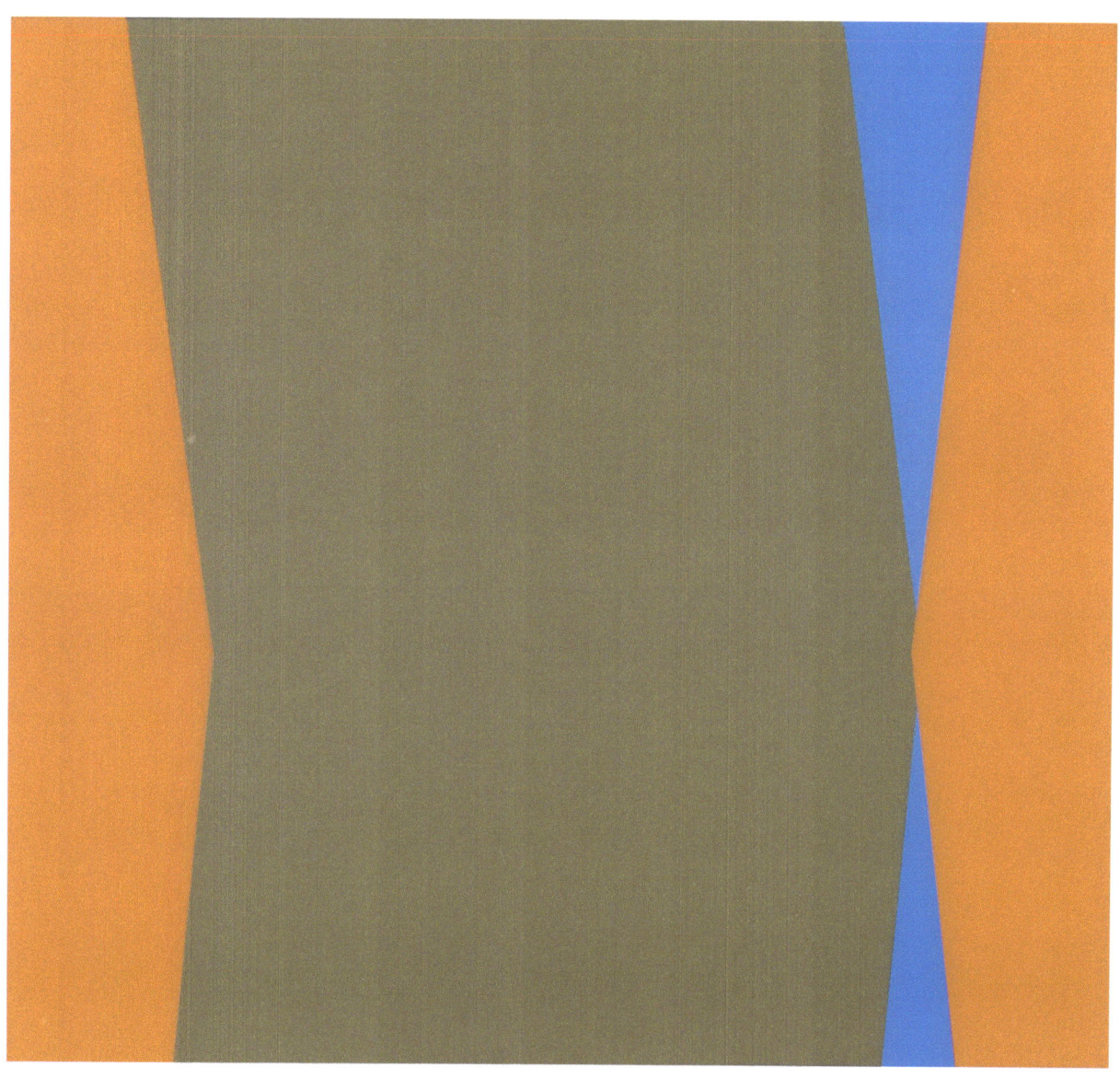

Form with Blue, 1972
Acrylic on canvas, 40.5 x 44 in.
Artists Archives of the Western Reserve

Opposite:
The Sky Beyond Phase B, 1969
Acrylic on canvas, 42 x 50 in.
Artists Archives of the Western Reserve

The Sky Beyond Phase B #8, 1982
Acrylic on canvas, 54 x 52 in.
Artists Archives of the Western Reserve

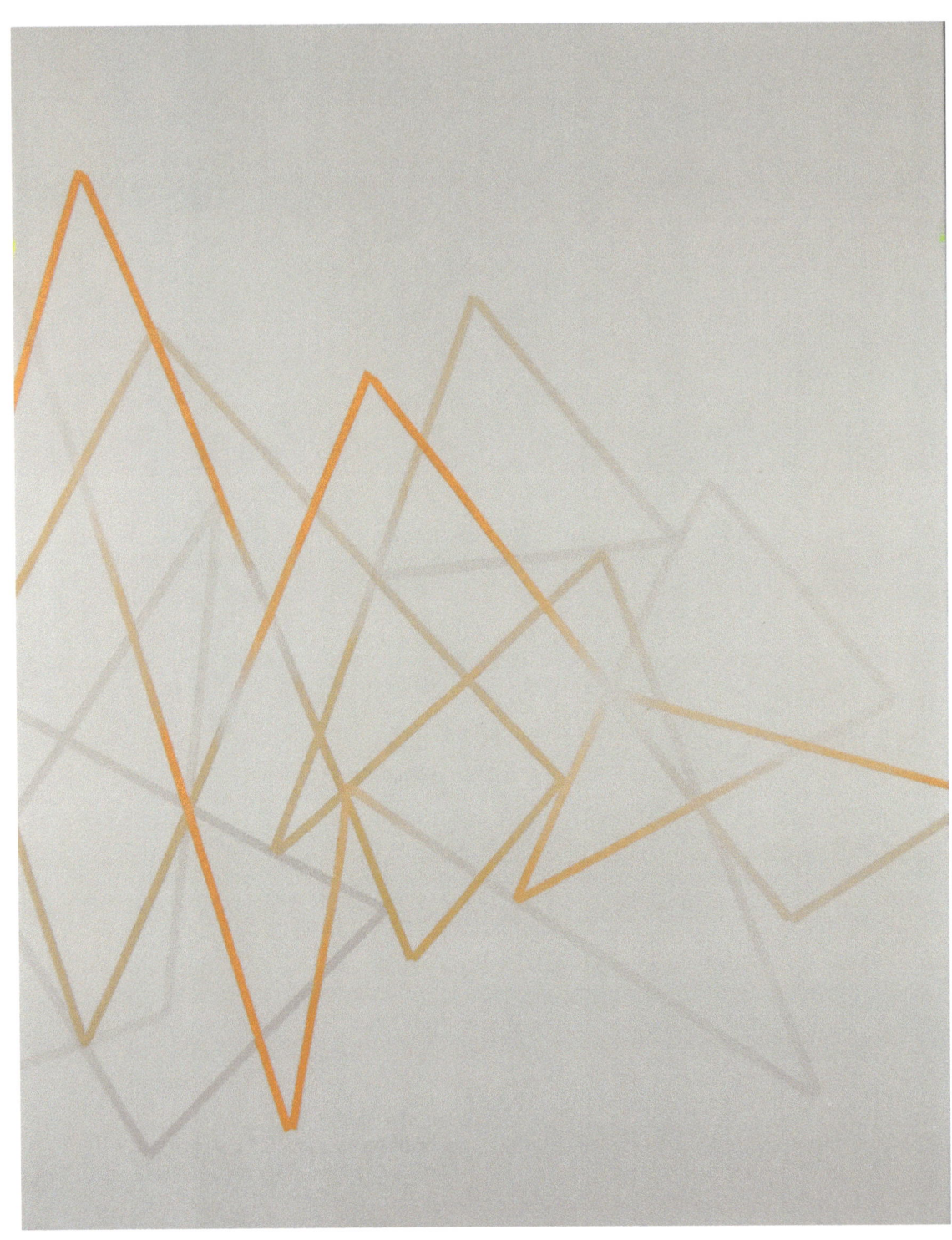

Configuration Series II, Grey 2, 1974
Acrylic on canvas, 60 x 48 in.
Artists Archives of the Western Reserve

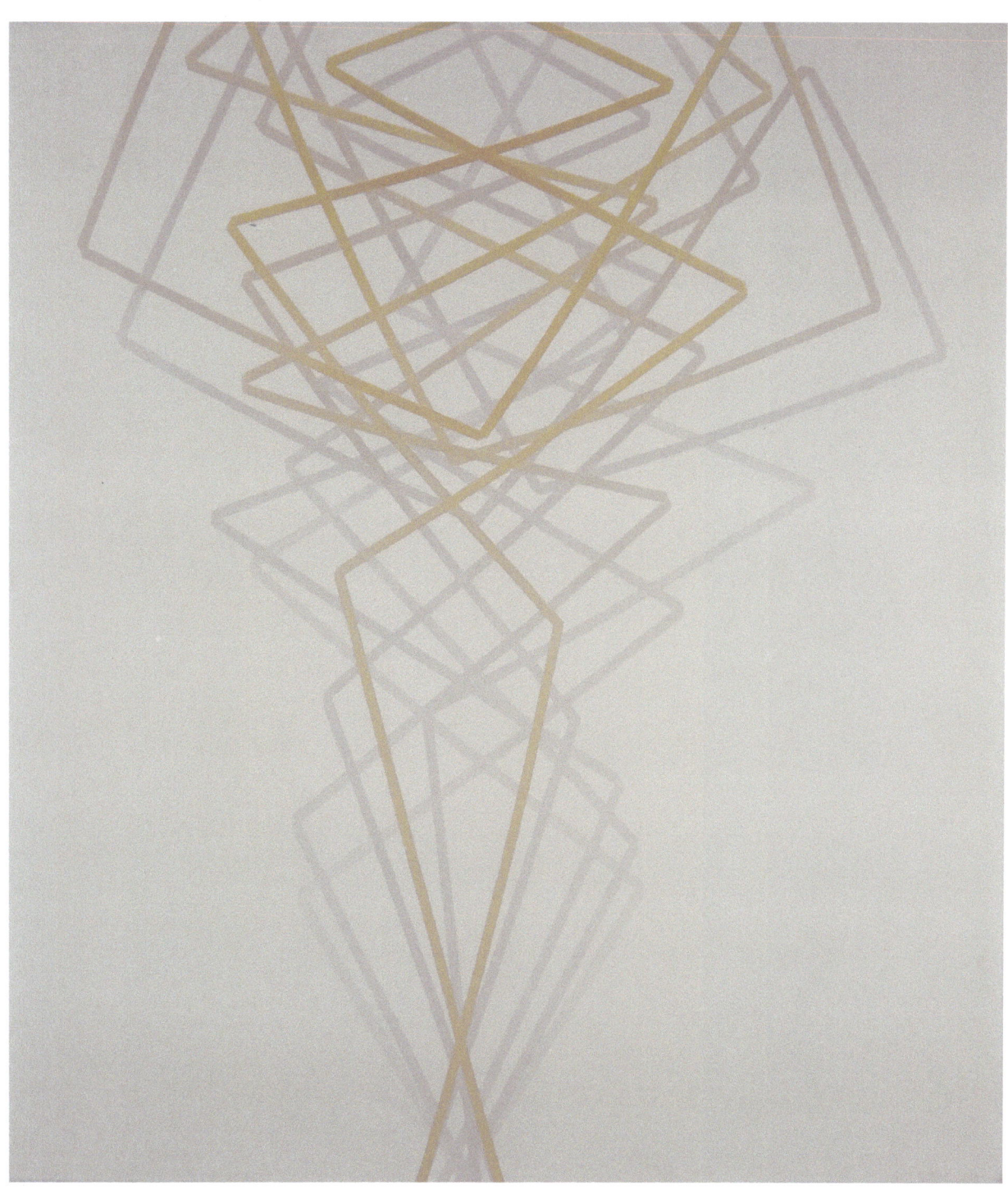

Configuration Series III, Grey 5, 1977
Acrylic on canvas, 60 x 48 in.
Artists Archives of the Western Reserve

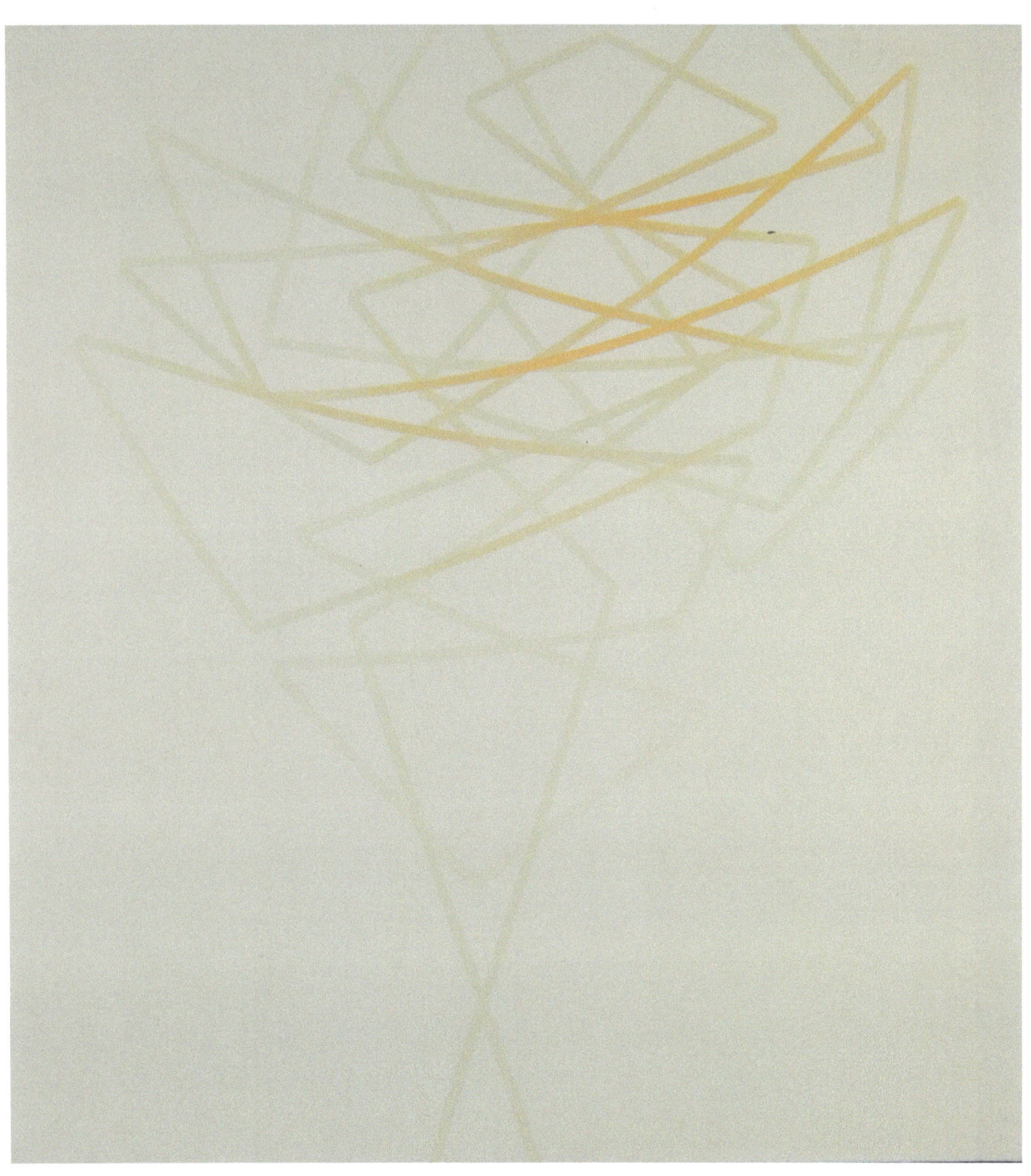

Configuration Series III, Off White 2, 1977
Acrylic on canvas, 54 x 48 in.
Artists Archives of the Western Reserve

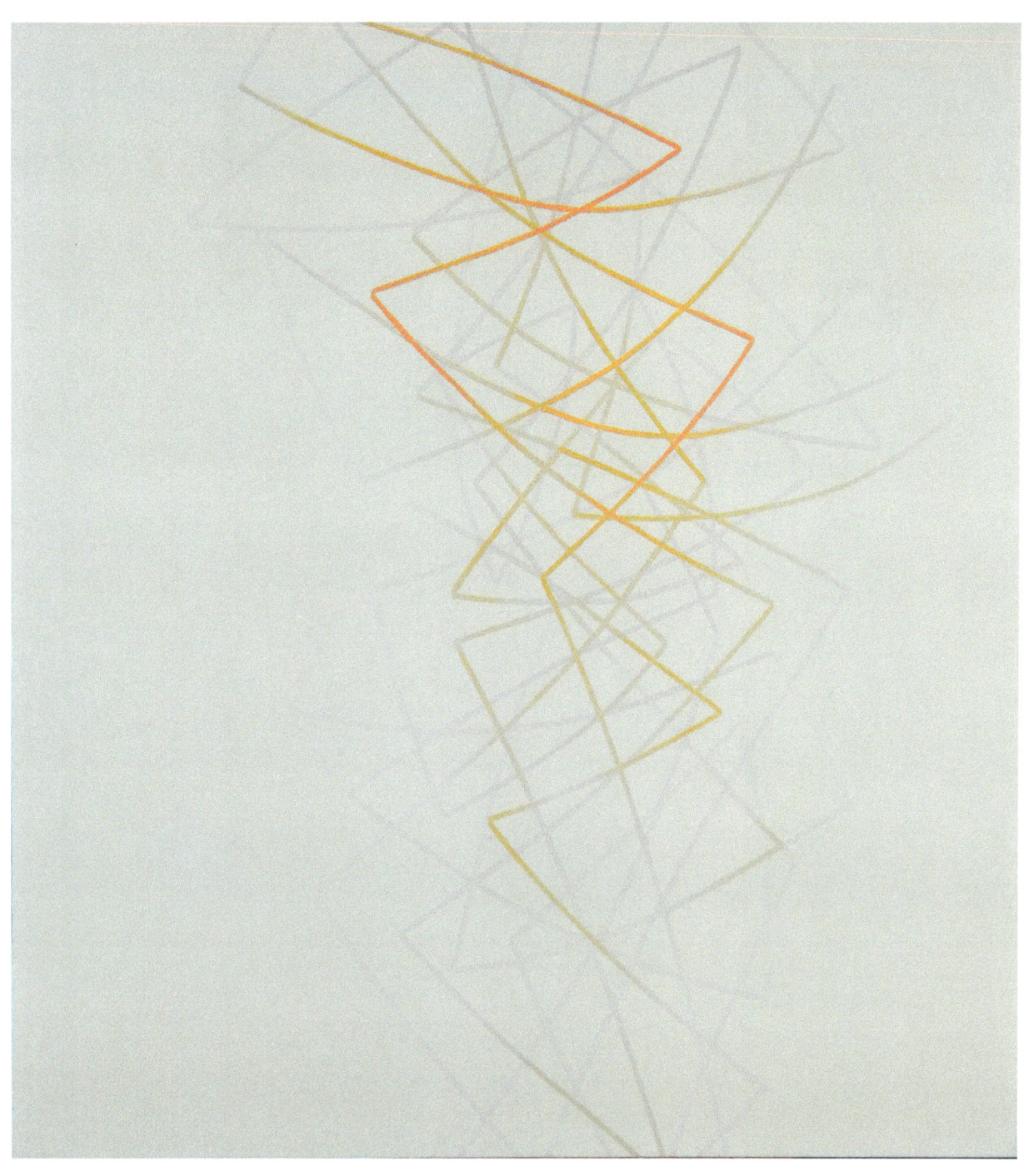

Configuration Series III, White, 1975
Acrylic on canvas, 48 x 44 in.
Artists Archives of the Western Reserve

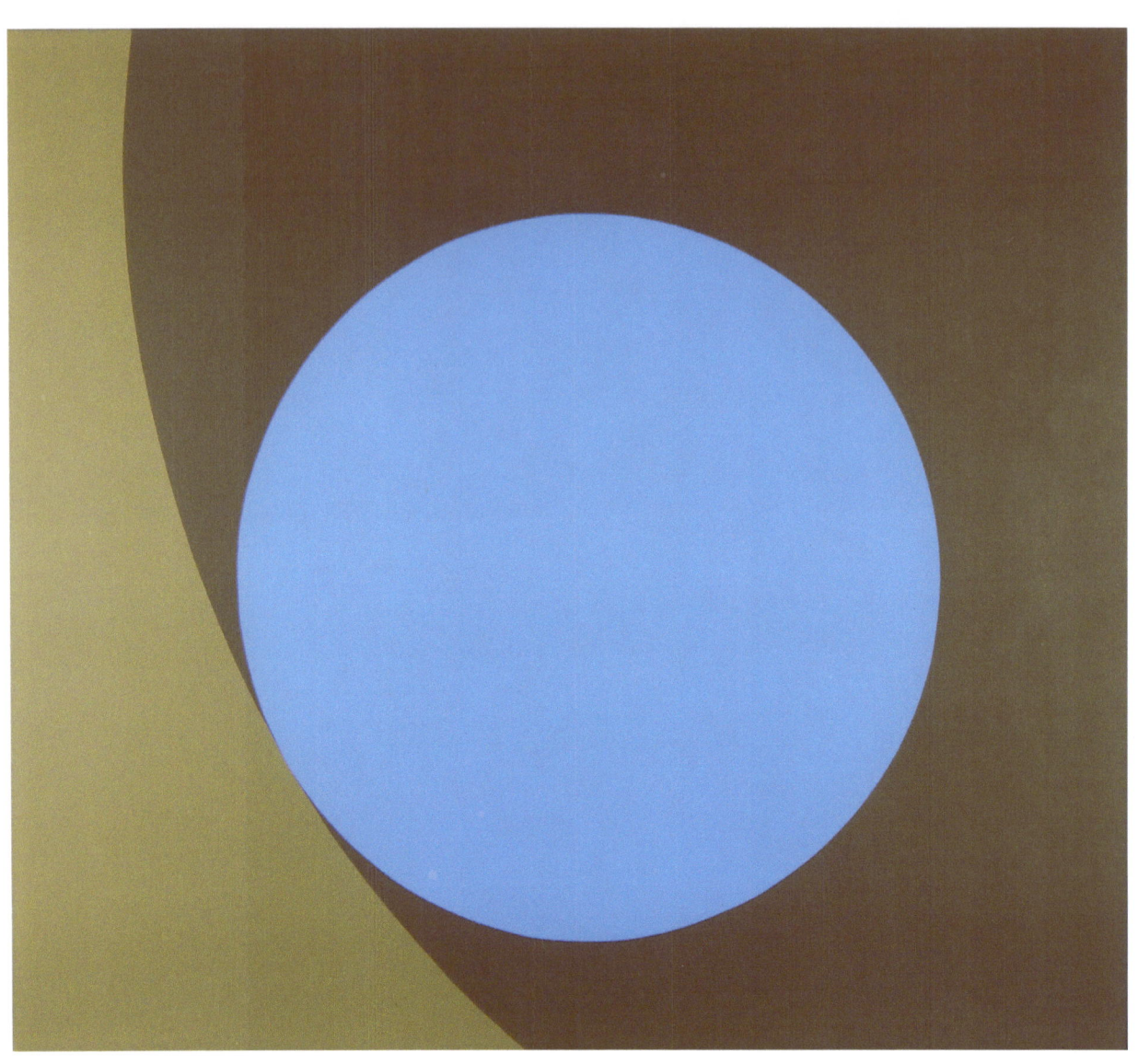

Circle Form #16, 1980
Acrylic on canvas, 48 x 54 in.
Artists Archives of the Western Reserve

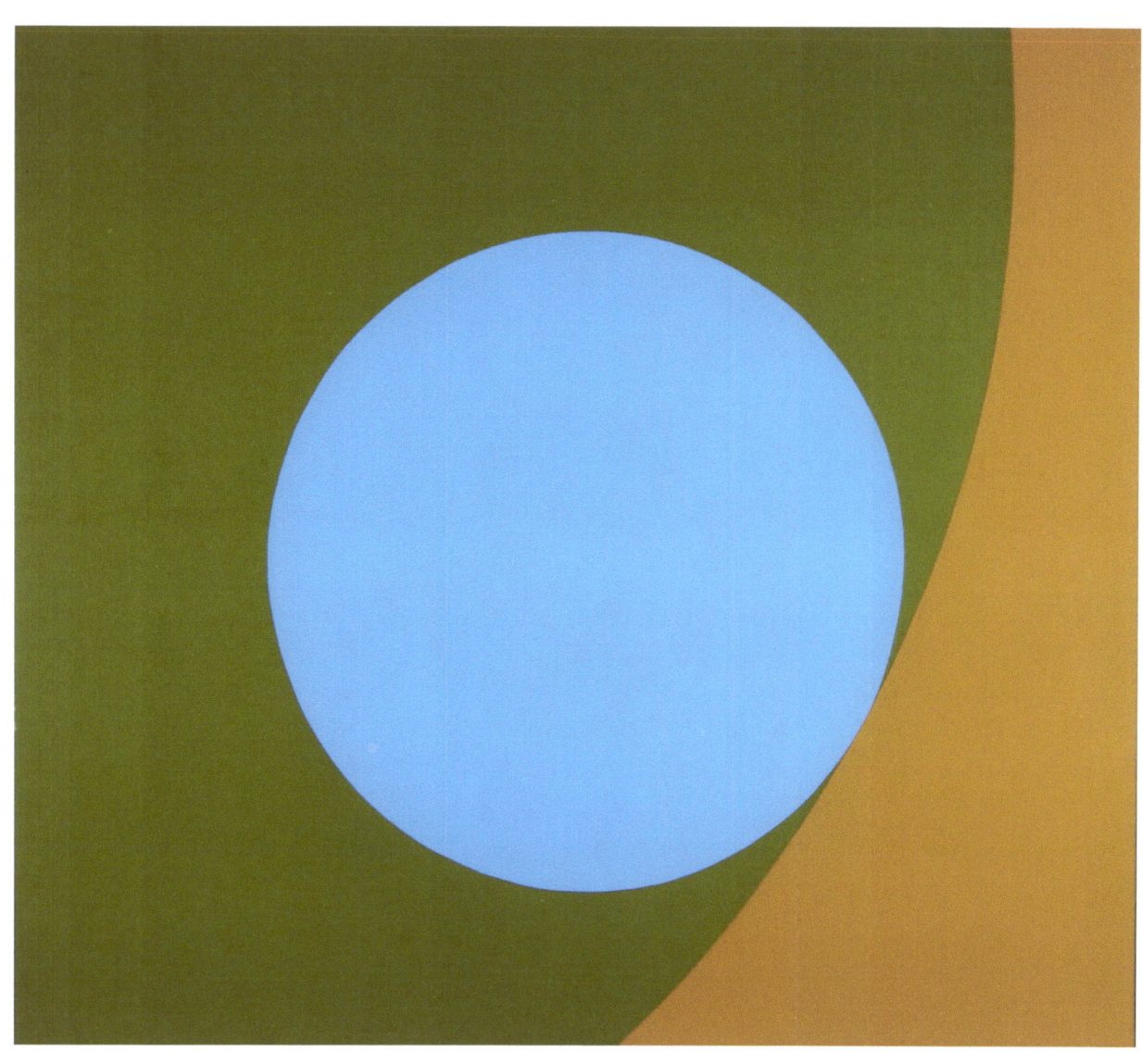

Circle Form #20, 1980
Acrylic on canvas, 48 x 54 in.
Artists Archives of the Western Reserve

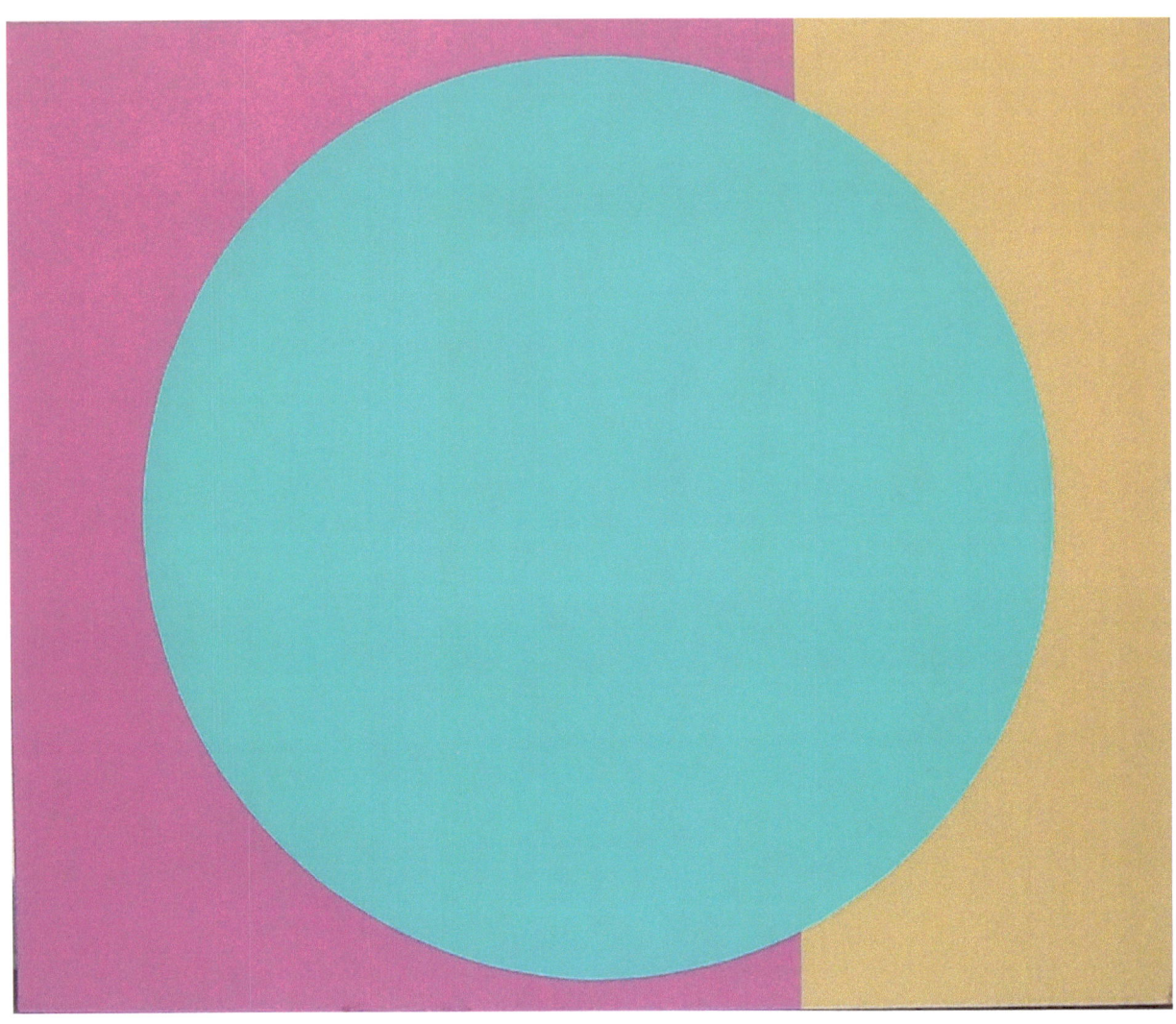

Circle Form Phase B, 1981
Acrylic on canvas, 42 x 50 in.
Artists Archives of the Western Reserve

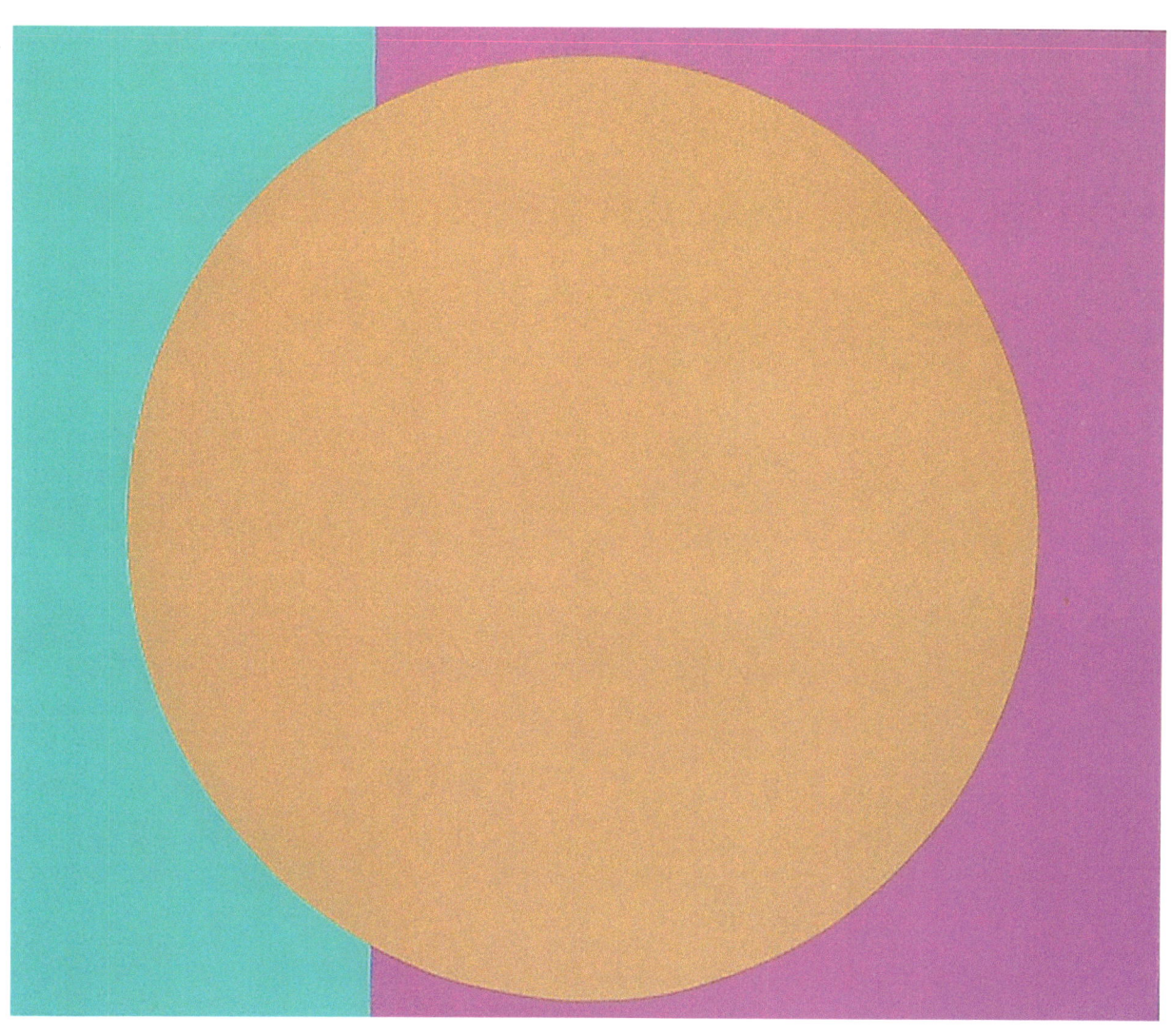

Circle Form Phase B #2, 1981
Acrylic on canvas, 42 x 50 in.
Artists Archives of the Western Reserve

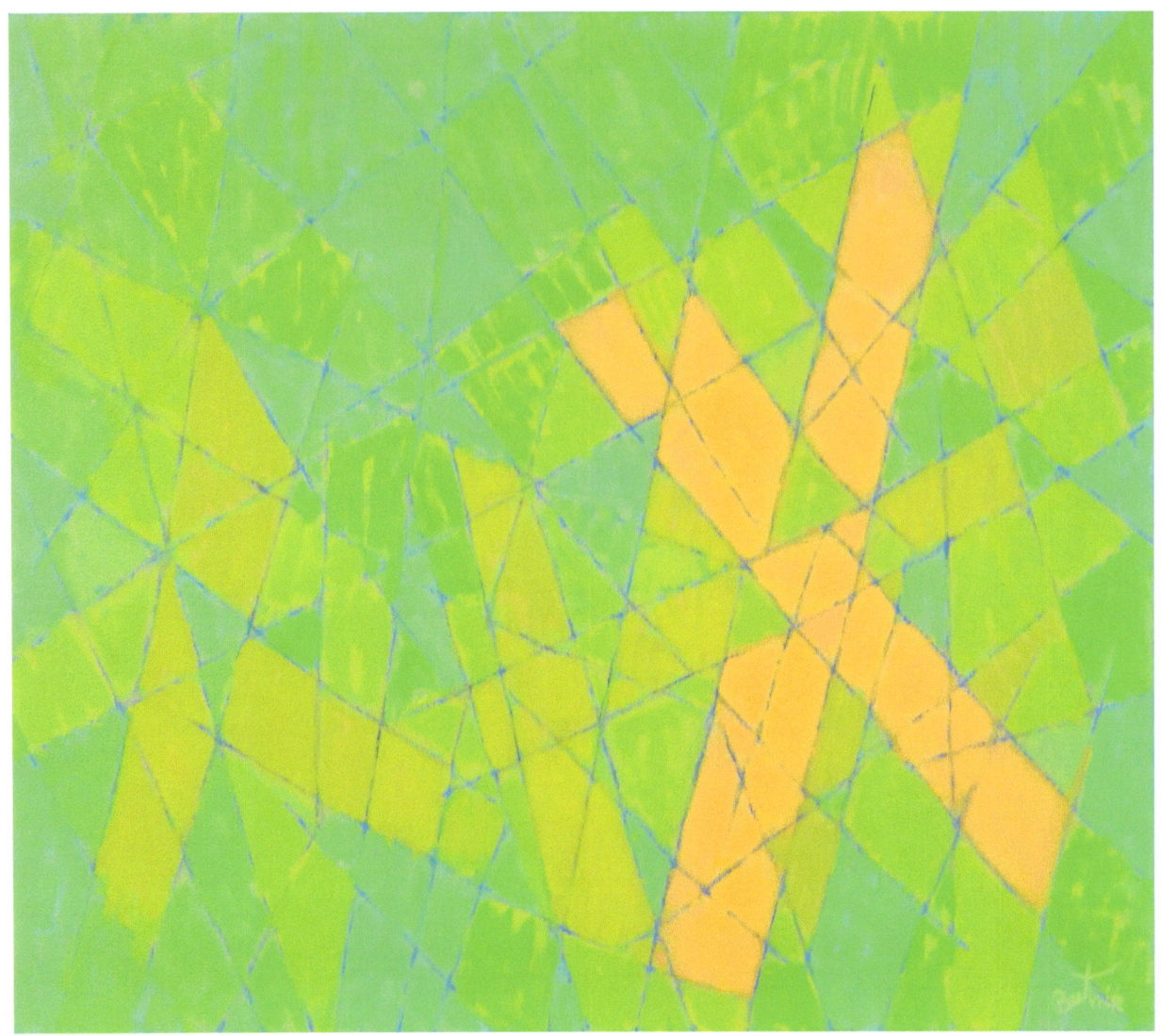

Untitled C3, 1990
Oil on canvas, 26 x 30 in.
Artists Archives of the Western Reserve

Opposite:
Untitled C1, 1990
Oil on canvas, 30.5 x 31 in.
Artists Archives of the Western Reserve

Untitled C6, 1992
Oil on canvas, 28.5 x 34 in.
Artists Archives of the Western Reserve

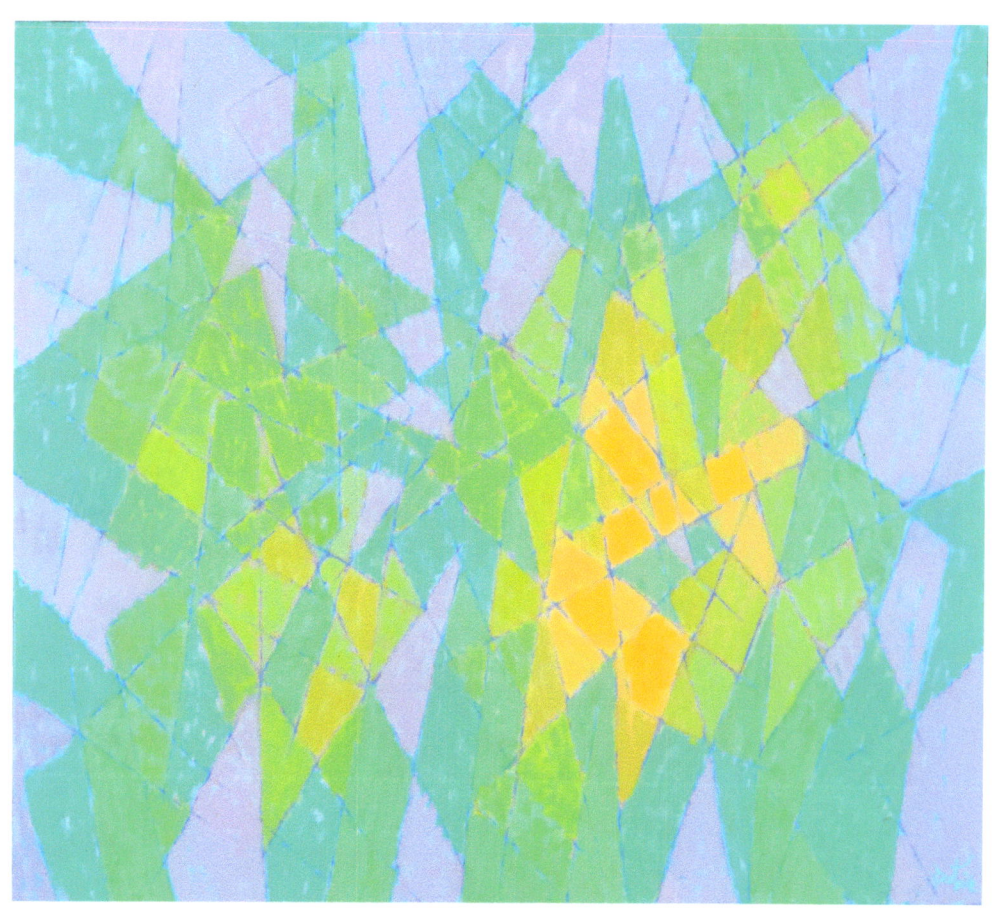

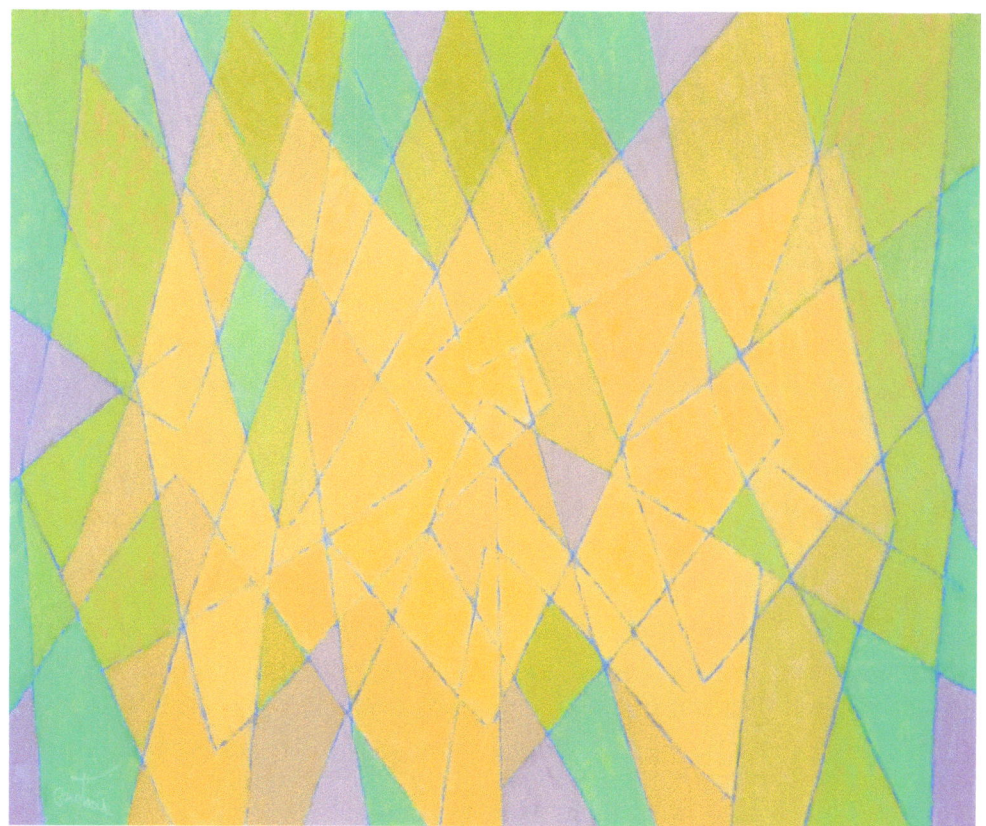

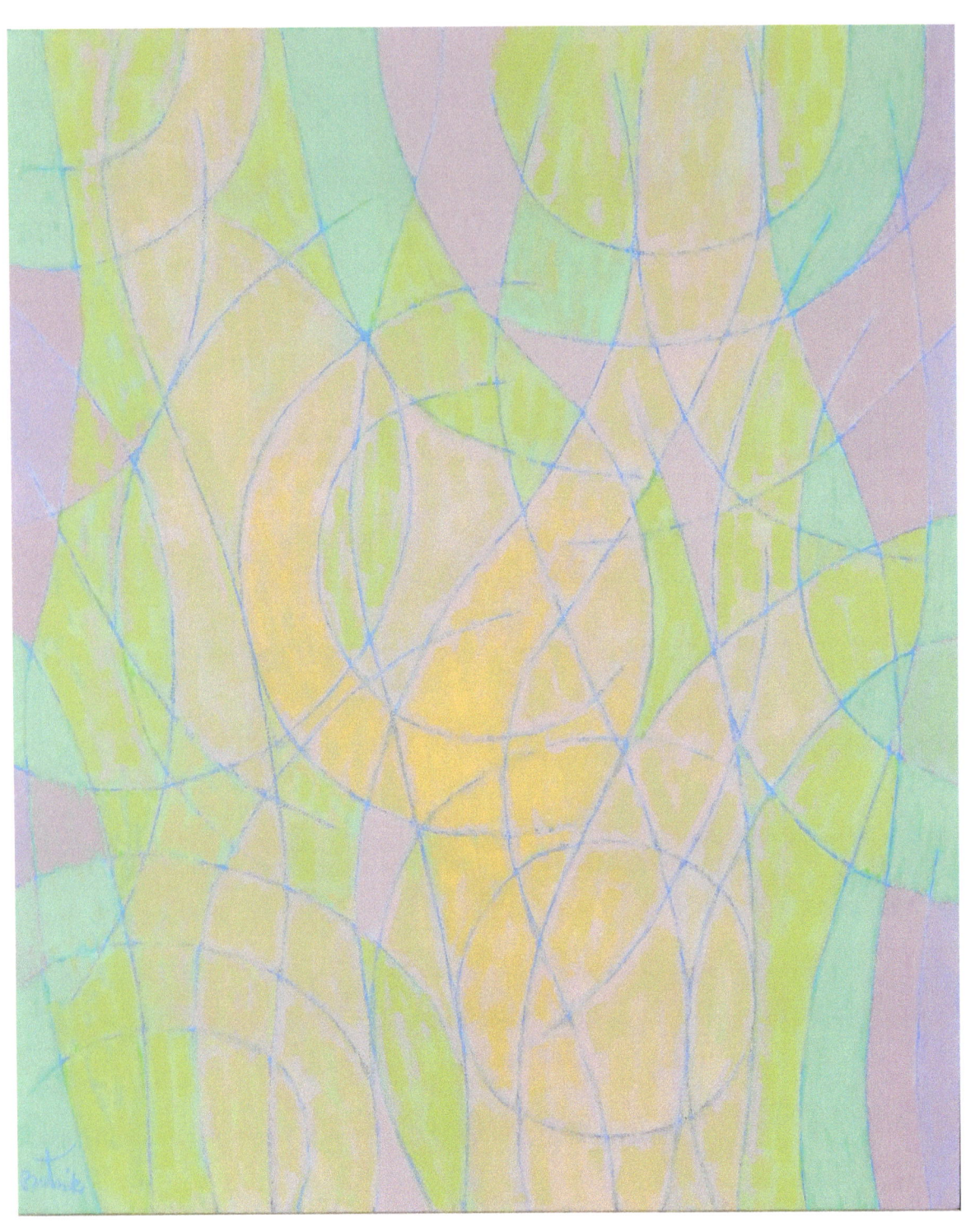

Untitled C3, 1990
Oil on canvas, 30.5 x 26.25 in.
Artists Archives of the Western Reserve

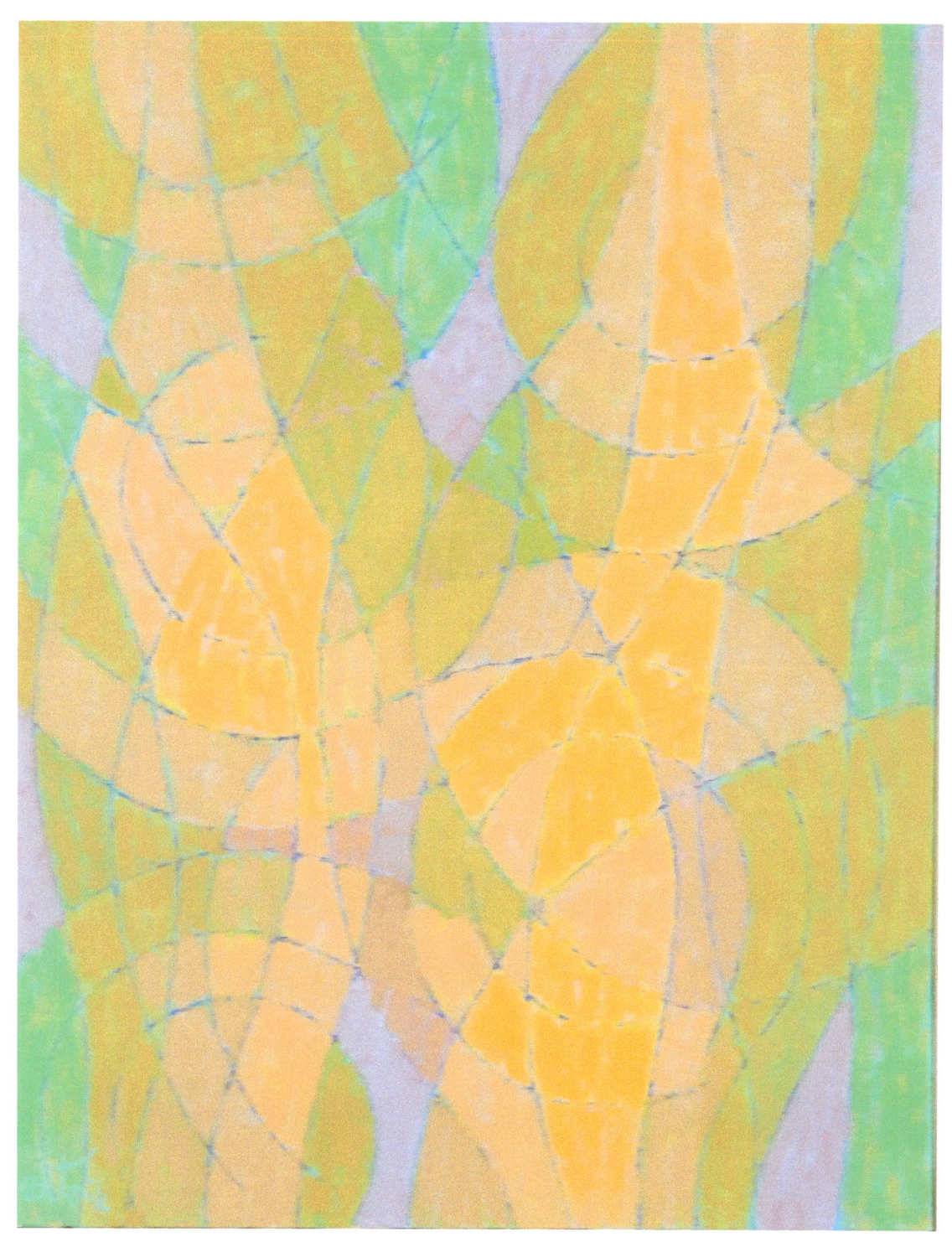

Untitled C4, 1990
Oil on canvas, 30 x 24.5 in.
Artists Archives of the Western Reserve

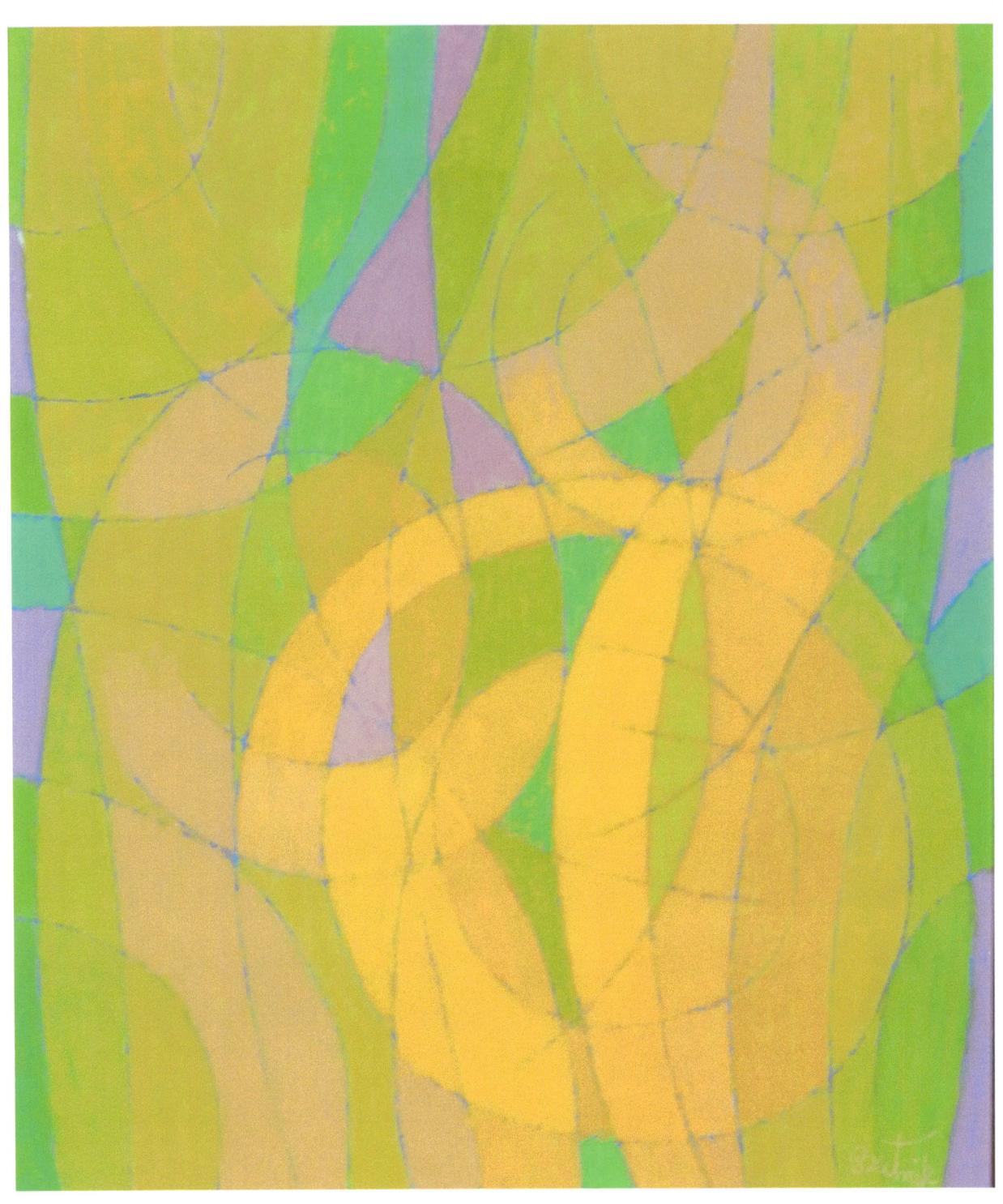

Untitled C8, 1991
Oil on canvas, 30.5 x 26.5 in.
Artists Archives of the Western Reserve

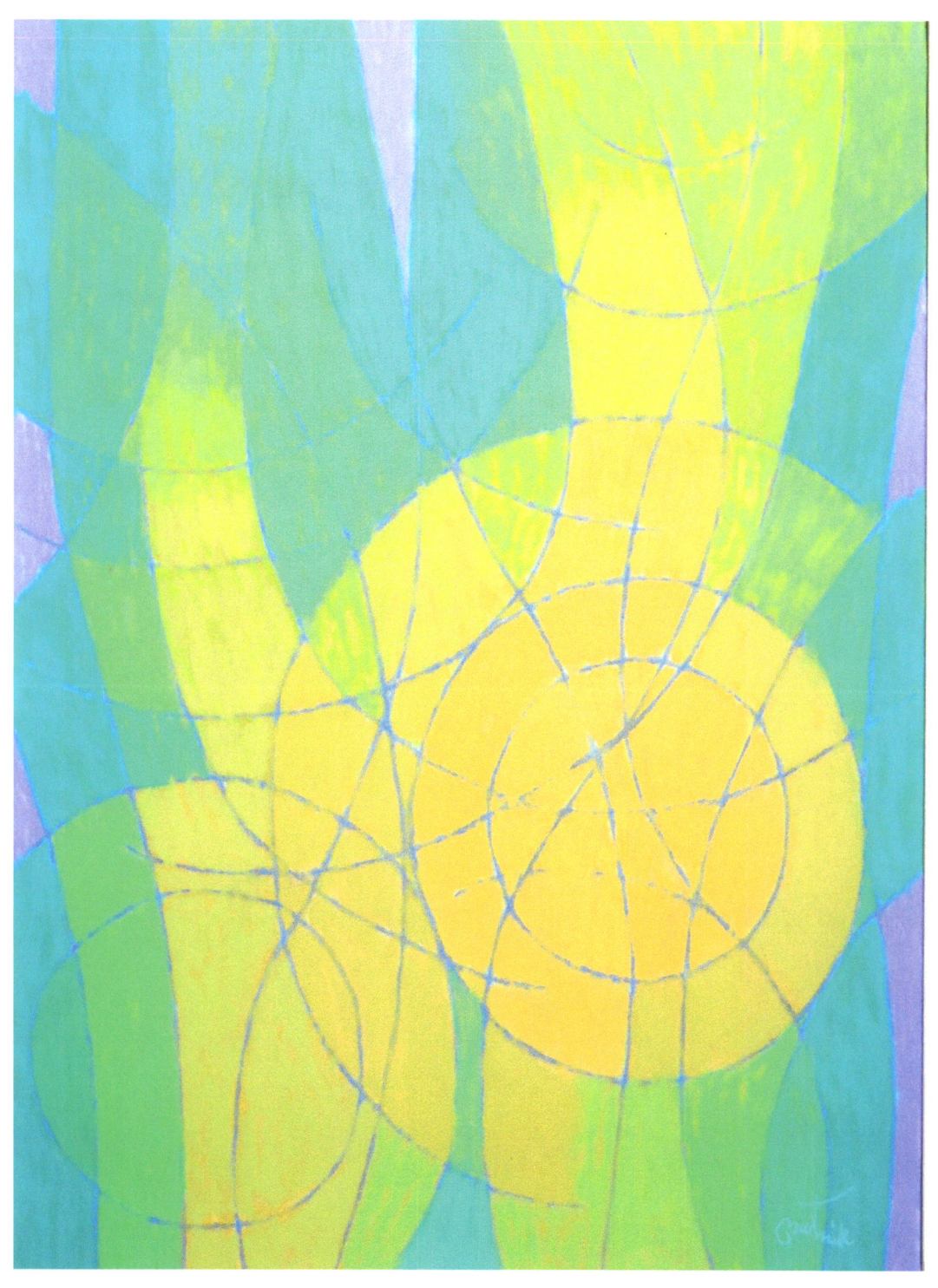

Untitled, 1991
Acrylic on canvas, 30.5 x 22.5 in.
Artists Archives of the Western Reserve

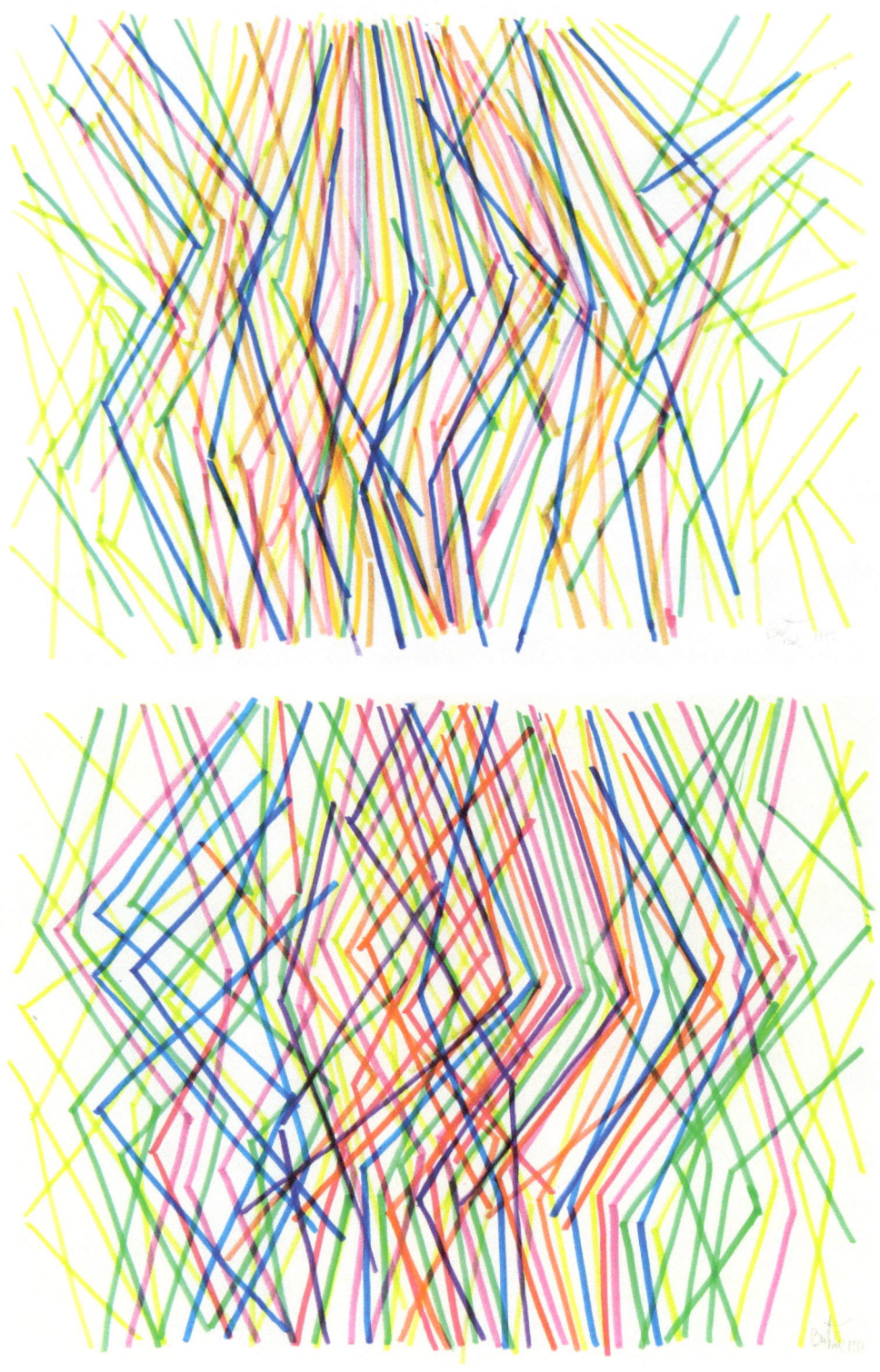

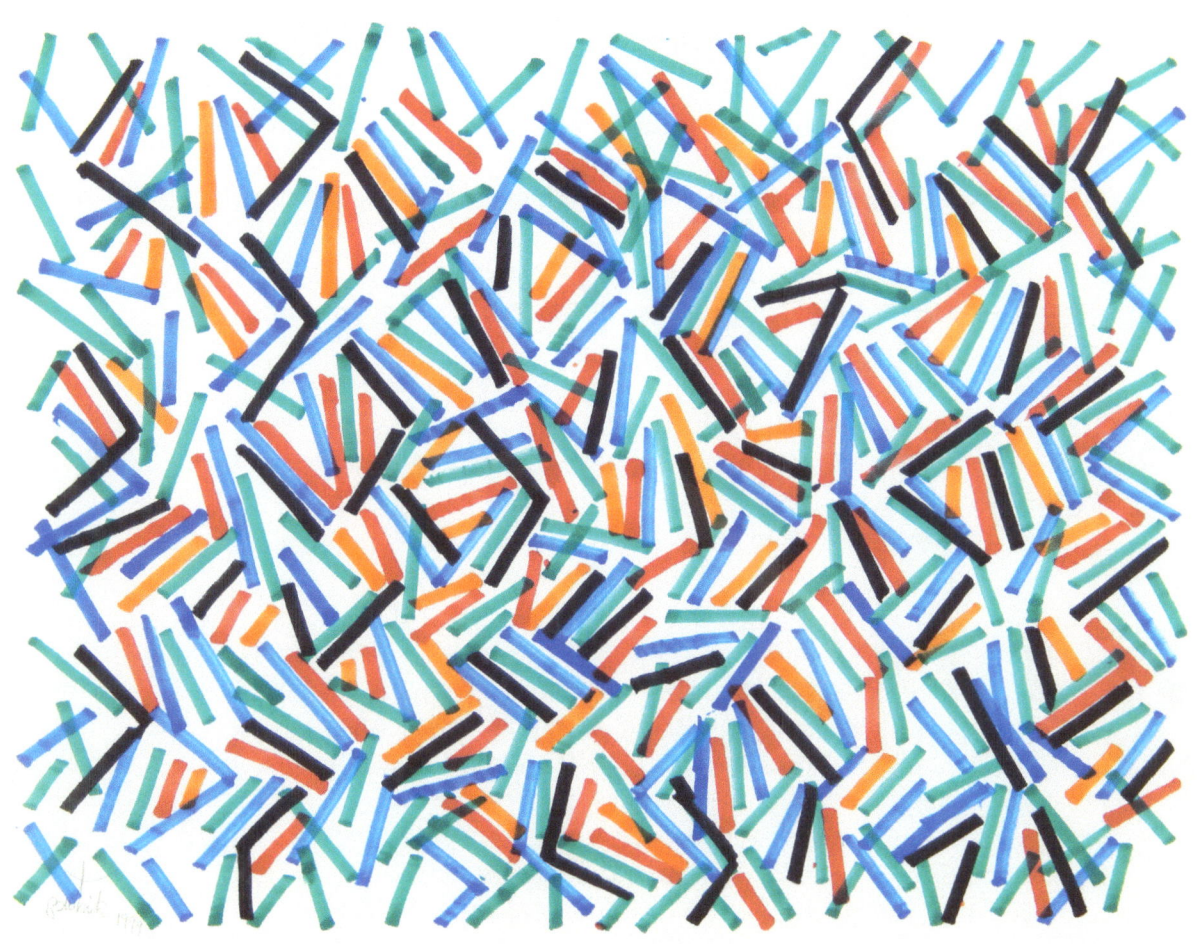

Untitled V20, 1999
Felt-tip marker on paper, 17 x 23 in.
Artists Archives of the Western Reserve

Opposite:
Untitled, 1997
Felt-tip marker on paper, 17 x 23 in.
Artists Archives of the Western Reserve

Untitled, 1997
Felt-tip marker on paper, 17 x 23 in.
Artists Archives of the Western Reserve

Chronology

1920	Born, Cleveland, Ohio
1938	Attended evening classes at the Cleveland School of Art as a high school senior
1939-41	Student, Cleveland School of Art
1941-45	Served with the Army Air Force as an artist in the Training Aids Department
1942-71	Exhibits in 17 *May Shows* at Cleveland Museum of Art during this period
1943	*Annual Midyear Show*, Butler Institute of American Art, Youngstown, Ohio
1944-45	*Army Art* (Ninth Service Command), San Francisco Museum of Art, First Prize & Honorable Mention
1944-47	Resumed studies at Cleveland School of Art, graduating in 1947
1947-50	Lived in Taos, New Mexico
1949	*Annual Midyear Show*, Butler Institute of American Art, Youngstown, Ohio
1950-55	Lived in New York City
1951	*May Show*, Cleveland Museum of Art, Honorable Mention Traveling Exhibition of Oils by Cleveland Artists, Cleveland Museum of Art
1955-56	Travels in England, France, Holland, Sweden and Denmark
1956	Returns to Cleveland
1957	*Art USA*, Madison Square Garden, New York *May Show*, Cleveland Museum of Art, Honorable Mention
1958-59	Traveling Exhibition of Oils by Cleveland Artists, Cleveland Museum of Art
1959	*May Show*, Cleveland Museum of Art, First Prize, Painting Traveling Exhibition of Oils by Cleveland Artists, Cleveland Museum of Art
1960	Group Show, Jewish Community Center, Cleveland, Ohio, First Prize *Annual Midyear Show*, Butler Institute of American Art, Youngstown, Ohio Traveling Exhibition of Oils by Cleveland Artists, Cleveland Museum of Art
1961-62	Traveling Exhibition of Work by Artists of the Western Reserve, Cleveland Museum of Art
1964-65	Traveling Exhibition of Work by Artists of the Western Reserve, Cleveland Museum of Art
1965	*Annual Midyear Show*, Butler Institute of Art, Youngstown, Ohio
1968	Cincinnati Zoo Arts Festival, Ohio, Cash Award *6 Ohio Artists*, Contemporary Arts Center, Cincinnati, Ohio
1969	*Third Annual Invitational*, Intown Club, Cleveland, Ohio
1970	*Small Works*, New Gallery (Center for Contemporary Art), Cleveland, Ohio *Cuyahoga College Invitational*, Cleveland, Ohio, First Prize Visual Arts Advisory Panel, Ohio Arts Council
1971	Saalfield & Sundell Collections, Mansfield Art Center, Ohio
1974	*Great American Paintings*, Walker Art Museum, Bowdoin College, Brunswick, Maine One person exhibition, Bristol Art Museum, Rhode Island
1977	*Grids: Samuel Butnik, David Davis, John Pearson*, Mansfield Art Center, Ohio *First Annual Invitational Painting Show*, Beachwood Museum of Art, Ohio *Bratenahl Place Invitational Exhibit*, Ohio
1991	One person exhibition, Stocker Center Gallery, Lorain Community College, Elyria, Ohio
1992	*Retrospective Exhibition*, Coburn Gallery, Ashland University, Ohio
2004	Died

Train to Luke Field, Arizona, 1942
Watercolor on paper
ARTneo Collection, Gift of the artist

At Ease, 1943
Watercolor on paper
ARTneo Collection, Gift of the artist

Army 1945, 1945
Ink, watercolor on paper
ARTneo Collection, Gift of the artist

Streetcar to Santa Ana, 1945
Ink on board
ARTneo Collection, Gift of the artist

Chance, 1946
watercolor on paper
ARTneo Collection, Gift of the artist

Design and Creation, 1947
Watercolor on paper
ARTneo Collection, Gift of the artist

Taos 1947, 1947
Watercolor on paper
ARTneo Collection, Gift of the artist

Mid Winter Day, Taos, New Mexico, 1947
Casein on paper
ARTneo Collection, Gift of the artist

Mid Winter Day, Taos, New Mexico, No. 2, 1947
Casein on paper
ARTneo Collection, Gift of the artist

Arroyo, 1948
watercolor on paper
ARTneo Collection, gift of the artist

Taos 1948, No. 6, 1948
Watercolor on paper
ARTneo Collection, Gift of the artist

Taos 1948, No. 9, 1948
Watercolor on paper
ARTneo Collection, Gift of the artist

Valley Road 2, 1948
Casein on paper
ARTneo Collection, Gift of the artist

The Hills Beyond, 1948
Casein on paper
ARTneo Collection, Gift of the artist

Taos Vista, 1948
Acrylic on board
ARTneo Collection, Gift of the artist

Amsterdam, Holland, 1955
Ink on paper
ARTneo Collection, Gift of the artist

Amsterdam, Holland, 1955
Ink on paper
ARTneo Collection, Gift of the artist

Brussels, Belgium, 1955
Ink on paper
ARTneo Collection, Gift of the artist

Brussels, Belgium, 1955
Ink on paper
ARTneo Collection, Gift of the artist

Copenhagen, Denmark, 1955
Ink on paper
ARTneo Collection, Gift of the artist

Copenhagen, Denmark, 1955
Ink on paper
ARTneo Collection, Gift of the artist

Stockholm, Sweden, 1955
Ink on paper
ARTneo Collection, Gift of the artist

Stockholm, Sweden, 1955
Ink on paper
ARTneo Collection, Gift of the artist

Torremolinos, Spain, 1956
Ink on paper
ARTneo Collection, Gift of the artist

Torremolinos, Spain, 1956
Ink on paper
ARTneo Collection, Gift of the artist

Back of the Moon #2, 1963
Oil on linen
Artists Archives of the Western Reserve

The Sky Beyond #6, 1969
Acrylic on canvas
Artists Archives of the Western Reserve

The Sky Beyond #44, 1969
Acrylic on canvas
Artists Archives of the Western Reserve

The Sky Beyond Phase B, 1969
Acrylic on canvas
Artists Archives of the Western Reserve

The Sky Beyond #29, 1971
Acrylic on canvas
Artists Archives of the Western Reserve

Earth, Sky, Moon, Vista 4, 1972
Acrylic on canvas
ARTneo Collection, Gift of the artist

Earth, Sky, Moon, Vista 10, 1972
Acrylic on canvas
ARTneo Collection, Gift of the artist

Earth, Sky, Sun, Vista 6, 1972
Acrylic on canvas
ARTneo Collection, Gift of the artist

Earth, Sky, Sun, Vista 8, 1972
Acrylic on canvas
ARTneo Collection, Gift of the artist

Form with Blue, 1972
Acrylic on canvas
Artists Archives of the Western Reserve

The Sky Beyond #31, 1972
Acrylic on canvas
Artists Archives of the Western Reserve

Configuration Series II, Grey 2, 1974
Acrylic on canvas
Artists Archives of the Western Reserve

Configuration Series III, White, 1975
Acrylic on canvas
Artists Archives of the Western Reserve

Configuration Series III, Grey 5, 1977
Acrylic on canvas
Artists Archives of the Western Reserve

Configuration Series III, Off White 2, 1977
Acrylic on canvas
Artists Archives of the Western Reserve

Circle Form #16, 1980
Acrylic on canvas
Artists Archives of the Western Reserve

Circle Form #20, 1980
Acrylic on canvas
Artists Archives of the Western Reserve

Circle Form Phase B, 1981
Acrylic on canvas
Artists Archives of the Western Reserve

Circle Form Phase B #2, 1981
Acrylic on canvas
Artists Archives of the Western Reserve

The Sky Beyond #36, 1981
Acrylic on canvas
Artists Archives of the Western Reserve

The Sky Beyond #37, 1982
Acrylic on canvas
Artists Archives of the Western Reserve

The Sky Beyond Phase B #8, 1982
Acrylic on canvas
Artists Archives of the Western Reserve

Untitled C1, 1990
Oil on canvas
Artists Archives of the Western Reserve

Untitled C3, 1990
Acrylic on canvas
Artists Archives of the Western Reserve

Untitled C4, 1990
Oil on canvas
Artists Archives of the Western Reserve

Untitled, 1991
Acrylic on canvas
Artists Archives of the Western Reserve

Untitled C3, 1991
Oil on canvas
Artists Archives of the Western Reserve

Untitled C8, 1991
Oil on canvas
Artists Archives of the Western Reserve

Untitled C6, 1992
Oil on canvas
Artists Archives of the Western Reserve

Untitled, 1997
Felt-tip marker on paper
Artists Archives of the Western Reserve

Untitled, 1997
Felt-tip marker on paper
Artists Archives of the Western Reserve

Untitled V20, 1999
Felt-tip marker on paper
Artists Archives of the Western Reserve

www.ingramcontent.com/pod-product-compliance
Lightning Source LLC
Chambersburg PA
CBHW050857180526
45159CB00007B/2706